The
Southern Way

The regular volume for the Southern devotee

Kevin Robertson

Issue 42

www.crecy.co.uk

© 2018 Crécy Publishing Ltd
and the various contributors

ISBN 9781909328761

First published in 2018 by Noodle Books
an imprint of Crécy Publishing Ltd

All editorial submissions to:
The Southern Way (Kevin Robertson)
Conway
Warnford Rd
Corhampton
Hants SO32 3ND
Tel: 01489 877880
editorial@thesouthernway.co.uk

A CIP record for this book is available from the British Library

Publisher's note: Every effort has been made to identify and correctly attribute photographic credits. Any error that may have occurred is entirely unintentional.
In line with the new design the front cover image has changed from that originally advertised. All other information is unaffected.

Printed in England by LatimerTrend

Noodle Books is an imprint of
Crécy Publishing Limited
1a Ringway Trading Estate
Shadowmoss Road
Manchester M22 5LH

www.crecy.co.uk

Issue No 43 of THE SOUTHERN WAY
ISBN 9781909328778
available in July 2018 at £14.95

To receive your copy the moment it is released, order in advance from your usual supplier, or it can be sent post-free (UK) direct from the publisher:

Crécy Publishing Ltd

1a Ringway Trading Estate, Shadowmoss Road, Manchester M22 5LH

Tel 0161 499 0024

www.crecy.co.uk

enquiries@crecy.co.uk

Front cover:
The preserved 'T9' 4-4-0 seen as No 120 on the down through line at Eastleigh likely soon after restoration to the condition seen. Transferred from general use at Exmouth Junction shed in March 1961, it nevertheless remained 'on the books' and was sent to Eastleigh in November of the same year pending restoration. Entering the works, it emerged in March 1962 in the livery shown having also received a 'heavy casual' repair. In this form it worked specials as well as ordinary services until July 1963, after which its use was restricted to special trains only until October 1963. There followed a lengthy sojourn in store at various locations before emerging in steam again in 1983, appropriately on the Mid Hants Railway. Subsequent to this it has seen use/store/overhaul on various heritage lines throughout the country.

Rear cover:
LBSCR 'C3' 0-6-0 No 301. One of ten members of the type, No 301 was built at Brighton on June 1906 and lasted to become BR No 32301 until withdrawn in February 1951.

Title page:
This time on special duty. No 120 at the closed Winchester Chesil station sometime in 1963 at the head of the privately sponsored 'Wintonian' special. It is believed this working may have had something to do with what was then referred to as King Alfred's College (more recently renamed the University of Winchester.
E.A. Sollars

Contents

Introduction 4

William Stroudley's 'D' Tanks 6

Rebuilding Victoria at the Turn of the 19
    Nineteenth and Twentieth Century

LBSCR Rolling Stock 28
    Slip-coaches and an inspection saloon

The Lines and Stations Dr Beeching 33
    Did Not Close
    Part 1: 1841-1947

Ambulance Trains in War 42
    SE&CR

The Lost Archives of Stephen Townroe 58
    Part 7

Rebuilt..70
    The letters and comments pages

Greenwich Park *Revisited*....................................78

The Horton Hospital Railway...............................89

Observations at Eastleigh, 19 March 1966...........99

Introduction

I have been called to task recently, I will not say by whom, but shall we say a regular reader whose comments and judgement I greatly respect, who advises I am starting to 'pontificate' somewhat in these introductions.

It is likely a fair point but I will defend myself by responding that most journal editorials do likewise and being the editor I do have a certain advantage in being able to sit around and indeed comment on whatever subject happens to be in my mind at the time. To be fair, it is likely little different to those who will pass comment – perhaps I should say judgement – on their peers on the various internet forums. For this issue though I will restrict what follows to factual matters – but I will give no guarantee I will not return to other topics in the future!

So, instead of opinions I will look at the content of this and future issues. If you were to ask what is there to follow in this issue, the response will naturally be an invitation to take a look at the contents page, which will reveal all. However, I would certainly draw your attention to the first few articles, which all have a definite 'Brighton' flavour.

Regular readers will be aware we have been running a regular series titled 'The Lost Archives of Stephen Townroe' – with plenty more still to come – and indeed from the feedback I receive it is also extremely popular. Cast your mind back a bit further and the name Edward Wallis will also be recalled, with his own masterly collection of 'infrastructure'-type images in the period up to 1935, some of which have appeared in *SW* although the majority have been published separately in what is now a four-book series. The Wallis collection was accessed through the kind offices of David Wallis, the son, but who sadly passed away in 2016. The collection now resides with David's sister, whom I was privileged to meet in 2017, and consequent upon that meeting a fourth book in the 'Infrastructure' series, *Forgotten Railway Infrastructure* (ISBN 978-1909328723) was released in September 2017.

Like Stephen Townroe, Edward Wallis was one of those whose records were to a high standard but again, like 'SCT', there were gaps in the collection; negatives listed that were simply not there, broken, misplaced, loaned – whatever. It was thus with amazement that I was recently shown a large canvas carrier bag and two boxes containing yet more material from the Wallis archive, including this time a number of lantern slides.

All have been faithfully scanned, another 371 to be precise, some Southern, some other lines and some clearly copies of what we have seen already, while others are copies of copies. Not all are suitable for reproduction; as with any collection there are the brilliant, the passable and, shall we say, the not so good. But they do fill in a number of gaps and as such we look forward to deciding how best to display this new material. As an example, one follows after this narrative. Be assured I will keep readers informed.

Otherwise, as to the future, I can advise we plan articles on signalling, more on locomotive types, experimentation, reminiscences, a major work on the Salisbury–Exeter main line, contemporary magazine extracts, as well as the unusual. For most articles I rely upon a select few whose names will, of course, be familiar; that is not to say we do not welcome more but planning what is to appear in each issue is not always straightforward, so my apologies if it is usually only possible to confirm the likely content of just one issue forward.

A new feature for this issue is to advertise meetings of societies and groups with a Southern theme, so if you would like your meetings or gatherings mentioned, do please get in touch via the usual editorial contact. Please note though that as *SW* appears quarterly we do need to know some months ahead. As an example, the South Hampshire branch of the Southern Electric Group and the southern area of the Light Rail Transit Association hold joint meetings in Eastleigh. Anyone with an interest in railways and tramways is very welcome.

Meetings are held on the first Tuesday of every month, except July and August, at the Eastleigh Railway Institute in Romsey Road, starting at 19.30. This venue is close to the railway and bus stations, and ample parking is nearby. The charge is a £3 entry fee to cover costs. The 2018 programme for the period June to December is as follows:

3 Apr Mark Greening – slides from the Derek Pye collection, covering Hampshire and the surrounding area from the 1950s to the 1970s.

1 May Bob Hodges presents tramway videos of Vienna, Manchester, Granada, San Francisco and Crich.

5 Jun Members' slides. This will be slides, not digital.

4 Sep Martyn Davies brings another of his selections of railway slides.

2 Oct Paul Coles takes us on a tour of preserved trams in the British Isles.

6 Nov AGM followed by members' digital slides.

4 Dec We welcome David Brown, who will address us on Southern Electric trains, from 1939 to the present day.

Further information on the Southern Electric Group's south Hampshire branch is available from the secretary, John Goodrich, on 023 8067 0028, or visit www.southernelectric.org.uk. The LRTA area officer is Martin Petch, who can be contacted on 023 8077 4186 or via their website at www.lrta.org.

Trying to find: Colin Scott Morton?
If Colin reads this or anyone who can give a lead to contacting this gentleman could he please contact the Editor.

Kevin Robertson

LSWR No 0321 at Winchester (GWR) sometime after September 1900 when the engine was entered into the duplicate list and before subsequent withdrawal in February 1907. This was one of four of the Metropolitan tank type, Nos 319, 321-3, which were the mainstay of trains from Winchester to the LSWR after the DNS connection from Winchester to Shawford Junction had been established in October 1891 – hence the GWR coaches. (GWR engines did not work south of Winchester until 1910 and even so some engine changing at Winchester continued until as late as 1952.) Although this (and a similar image showing another engine of the class on a train south of the GWR station at Winchester, see page 180 of Bradley's *An Illustrated History of LSWR Locomotives – The Early Engines* by Wild Swan) may well be familiar to some readers, we have deliberately taken the opportunity to use it again here as it also shows another interesting feature not apparent from previous reproductions. Here we have what is clearly the full extent of the original negative – this scanned from a lantern slide in the latest batch of images from the Wallis collection – see the introduction to this issue. As if to prove the point we have included the view right to its extreme edges. The point of interest is the concave appearance of the hillside here between the footbridge and tunnel mouth: the result of a major chalk fall of December 1891 just two months after the station had ceased to be a terminus. This explains the difference in the 'grassing over' between the deep cutting sides. Incidentally (and going back several hundred years), history has it that at least one public execution was carried out on what was St Giles Hill in the background. *Courtesy the Wallis archive*

William Stroudley's 'D' Tanks

Jeremy Clarke

As well as being what Brian Haresnape describes as an able and professional engineer, William Stroudley was also very much an artist. Any of those who have seen any of his locos pictured or, better still, in preservation, even those enthusiasts who have little interest in the LBSCR or any railway south of the Thames, would agree with that. The minute 'A' class 'Terriers' and the ground-breaking 'B1', the 'Gladstones', are the best known of all the engines he introduced to the Brighton. But I would suggest the 'D' class 0-4-2T of 1873 epitomised his approach to locomotive design, for they were exactly suited to the work for which they were designed; tough, durable and in some cases of remarkable longevity.

Born at Sandford-upon-Thames in Oxfordshire on 6 March 1833, Stroudley went as a boy to work alongside his father at a local paper mill before spending time in Birmingham with various firms concentrating mainly on the manufacture and erection of stationary engines. By the time he was 20, in 1853, he came under the influence of Daniel Gooch at Swindon, though a year later he was offered a position in Australia. However, he was dissuaded from emigrating and instead went to the Great Northern at Peterborough under the command of Archibald Sturrock, another Swindon 'product', although here he reported directly to Charles Sacré, later Locomotive Superintendent of the Manchester, Sheffield & Lincolnshire Railway.

A few years later, at the age of just 28, he was appointed manager of the Edinburgh & Glasgow Junction Railway's Cowlairs Works in Glasgow. Shortly afterwards, Samuel Johnson also came to work for that company but he was senior to Stroudley. Despite the fact both in time produced aesthetically beautiful engines in luscious liveries, the two soon developed an intense dislike of one another. Perhaps the fall out was due to their artistic temperaments or, more likely, each considered the other an engineering rival.

'Belgravia' class 2-4-0 No 205 *Kensington* at Battersea. This and the five sister engines in the class were built by William Stroudley using sets of frames inherited from his predecessor, John Chester Craven. The design was similar to a pair of 2-4-0 tender engines built by Stroudley when he was in charge at Cowlairs on the Edinburgh and Glasgow railway in the 1860s. Variously renumbered in the ensuing years, all six had been withdrawn by 1902, No 605 as she was at the time ceasing service in 1901. This and the other sepia LBSCR images in this issue are from the collection of the late R.C. Riley.

0-6-0 No 77, one of six of the LBSCR 'C' class built under Stroudley's auspices at Brighton between March 1873 and November 1874. (Twelve others were constructed by Messrs Kitson & Co. at the same time and with two earlier engines of the type having also been erected at Brighton in 1871.) Intended for freight duty, they were poor steaming engines and were superseded by his 'C1' 0-6-0 type in the 1880s.

Stroudley's next opportunity came in July 1865 when he was appointed Locomotive, Carriage & Wagon Superintendent of the Highland Railway, newly-formed by amalgamations. At first he may very well have considered himself fortunate for there were no fewer than thirty-one applicants for the post, but financially the Highland was a very poor company and gave Stroudley little scope to express himself, although he rebuilt some 'singles' into successful 2-4-0s and updated the Lochgorm workshops. It was not until 1869 that he produced his first Highland engine, albeit a small shunting 0-6-0T loco that contained a number of second-hand parts including the wheels and boiler barrel. However, it carried not just the beautifully lined out ochre livery that was to become his later trademark but also the typical cab with the toolbox behind it. (The bunker was on the offside forward of the cab.)

After only a short time in Scotland, he went to Brighton to succeed John Chester Craven, of whom Hamilton Ellis wrote ' … [nobody] could find an atom of amiability or humour in [his] character …' (Bill Aves – see bibliography – rather mildly describes the regime under Craven as idiosyncratic.) There could be no greater contrast between the two for Craven was 'always harsh and bigoted' and also 'sometimes violent and cruel'. But Stroudley, although a martinet in his own way, had already proved himself an excellent man-manager and followed Gooch's practice of knowing every man who worked for him. Perhaps that showed best in each engine being allocated to a particular driver, whose name and the mileage run was then painted inside the cab front. Although no less a

Victorian than Craven in matters of discipline, he soon came to be regarded as a just man and a considerate chief. In such ways Stroudley gained more than mere respect from his staff.

Among Stroudley's first essays, during which time he was also concerned with modernising and redesigning the layout of Brighton Works, was the reconstruction of some Craven 'singles' that had come from Robert Stephenson in 1864. One of these re-emerged as the famous Sussex, still a 'single' but with a new and bigger boiler, having his favoured Salter safety valves on the dome and the copper-capped chimney that became his standard. She was the only one of her class but was renowned as a fast and powerful engine.

More significantly perhaps, Stroudley found himself with a pair of 0-4-2Ts to Craven's design but with only a minimum of work started on them. Using some of those prepared parts, he changed the design from that of a double-framed saddle tank to inside-framed engines with side tanks. Numbered 18 and 21, they were without cabs but had the copper-capped chimney. Following the derailment of No 21 while the pair were engaged on London suburban services, Stroudley modified the springing and sent the engine variously to Brighton, Eastbourne and Horsham sheds. It quickly became evident that these postings and their subsequent work were part of a trial as Stroudley pursued his ideas for building engines with this wheel arrangement. The pair were later renumbered respectively 373 and 467, the former withdrawn in May 1886 while the latter soldiered on for another two years.

Also from the first batch was No 3 *Battersea* dating from December 1873. The others were: No 1 *Sydenham*, November 1873; No 2 *Wandsworth*, December 1873; No 4 *Mickleham*, January 1874; No 5 *Streatham*, January 1874; and No 6 *Wimbledon*, January 1874.) Note the massive wooden brake blocks. No 3 had the shortest life of any of the class, being withdrawn in December 1903 with four more following the next year. According to the RCTS, the reason for withdrawal was in all cases corrosion of the framing below the footplate and bunker due to frequent hosing down of the footplate and damping of the coal. In addition, most were by now also in need of new cylinders and fireboxes.

Having introduced his 'C' class 0-6-0 goods engines, the 'Jumbos', and completed the six 2-4-0 'Belgravias', whose frames Craven had of necessity ordered from Messrs Avonside simply because Brighton was incapable of cutting the plates, attention turned to the 'A' class 0-6-0T engines, the 'Terriers'. The first six were introduced between September and December 1872. (Batches then followed to September 1880, by which time fifty engines were in service.) So, with the start made on solving the problem of working inner-suburban trains over relatively poor track with frequent stops, Stroudley turned to designing an engine to take the place of the various Craven specimens handling the outer suburban work, where stops were less frequent and speeds rather higher. In the past, Craven had generally preferred tender engines for such services although Stroudley decided to make matters simpler by using tank engines instead, thus eliminating the need for turning at the end of each journey. Thus this is where the earlier trials with No 21 now bore fruit as he settled on a 0-4-2T type wheel arrangement.

The 'D' class appeared in late 1873, No 1, *Sydenham,* the first of a lot of six, on 25 November, the rest of the lot by the year's end. The inside cylinders were 17in × 24in, driving wheels 5ft 6in and the trailing wheel beneath the cab, the latter to a large 4ft 6in diameter. This became the general diameter for Stroudley's trailing and tender wheels, though his trademark inside-framed tender had yet to appear; but here

was an indication of his intent on standardising parts to minimise the number of patterns required, to reduce both the costs of construction and, perhaps most importantly, capital tied up in a wealth of different spares.

This approach was something quite new to the Brighton Board, which had only just begun to question Craven's completely opposite view, that specific engines had to be designed for specific work in specific places. It was as though he had an almost childlike delight in designing engines for their own sake, use of anything 'standard' thus being an anathema to him. (It has to be said there was nothing otherwise childlike about Craven!) but I wonder if the Board would have permitted continued use of Stroudley's 'Improved Engine Green' livery with its expensive and involved lining out had such savings not been made.*

The 15ft wheelbase of the 'D' was divided 7ft 7in + 7ft 5in, the overall length of the engine being 31ft 7½in. The three-ring boiler, having a maximum diameter of 4ft with the dome on the third ring, contained a total heating surface of 933 sq ft, of which the firebox, with a grate area of 15¼ sq ft, contributed 88 sq ft. Pressure was 140psi which, at 85%, provided a tractive effort of 12,506lb.

The bunker held 1½ tons of coal and the tanks 860 gallons, making the engine weight in working order 38½ tons, of which 27 tons was adhesive, divided equally. One peculiarity to modern day eyes were the massive wooden brake blocks. Later batches

'Baynards' No 268 and the first of the class delivered with cast iron brake blocks in 1880. This is a post-1905 view, by which time the company initials had replaced the painted name on the side tanks and with the loco number also painted rather than having a cast plate fitted. (Do any of the original number plates survive?) The original print gives no idea as to the identity of the man stood on the footplate, although I think we can safely say it is not a member of the footplate crew. Note also the position of the bucket atop the side tank. This engine survived in traffic for forty-six years and was withdrawn in September 1926. *H.M. Madgwick collection*

The solitary 'D1x', originally to the conventional design as No 20 but seen here after rebuilding in 1910 using a Marsh boiler together with other modifications. It was also renumbered 79A as here – later taking the identification, 349, 216, B216 and finally 2216. The engine is fitted with coal rails, which increased the bunker capacity to 2¾ tons. It is believed all the engines, including of course this rebuild, were similarly fitted with coal rails, likely soon after 1900.

were equipped with cast iron blocks following improvements made to sanding gear in 1879. The first so equipped was No 268, *Baynards,* prior to delivery in June 1880. Some of the earlier members of the class were fitted retrospectively. Stroudley also provided screw reverse rather than the usual massive lever with its 'fixed' coarse notches, so making it possible for a driver to work his engine most economically.

Nine engines appeared in 1874, another nine in 1875 and twelve in 1876. With few exceptions these bore London suburban names. Now with thirty-six in traffic, numbered consecutively 1-36, real inroads could begin to be made into the more venerable and inefficient Craven outer-suburban motive power. No 15, *Silverdale,* of March 1875, was the first member of the class and in fact the first Brighton engine to have the driver's name and mileage painted in the cab. The first fitting of Westinghouse brake gear went to No 25, *Rotherfield.* All these engines and indeed the class as a whole were fitted with Stroudley's condensing system in which a proportion of the exhaust was turned back into the tanks to heat the feedwater. Feed pumps were thus required, as injectors – apparatus Stroudley would not touch – did not operate with hot water. (At this time the pumps were worked by eccentrics on the leading axle: hence it was not unknown to see an engine scurrying up and down the length of the

platform at, say, London Bridge, in order to top up the boiler! Weir feed pumps appeared rather later.)

In 1910 Marsh rebuilt No 20, *Carshalton,* with a boiler of 4ft 6in diameter, nevertheless of slightly reduced heating surface, although the pressure was raised to 170psi. The higher pitch demanded comparable changes to the cab roof and footplate. The weight also increased by 5 tons. The general opinion is that this was not an improvement, especially as the higher boiler pitch made the engine rather unsteady at anything over 40mph or thereabouts. No more received the treatment to become class 'D1x', which rather confirms the opinion. *Carshalton* was scrapped in 1934, although it is believed the boiler – or the shell at any rate – was recovered for further use.

The first of the thirty-six to meet the cutter's torch was No 3, *Battersea,* in 1903, and nine more had gone before the First World War. It is probable frame corrosion provided the cause for a proportion of withdrawals, although some of the cylinder blocks also turned out to be in poor condition, perhaps because of the chemistry of the iron involved. Marsh salvaged some pieces, particularly wheels, coupling and connecting rods and parts of the motion for reuse in the early members of the 'I1' class of 1907.

Exactly half the thirty-six came to the Southern, four of them, Nos 5, 6, 18 and 36, lasting into National ownership. No 6 of this lot, *Wimbledon,* was the first of the class to receive a Billinton

No 265 *Chipstead*, one of those built by Messrs Neilson & Co of Glasgow in May 1882, engaged on a typical suburban working – from the headcode this may well be a Crystal Place to London Bridge or Willow Walk (main line from Sydenham Junction) service or possibly a Shoredich and Peckham Rye 'ordinary train' see the excellent SEMG headcode page at www.semgonline.com/headcodes/sheadcodes/02.html. Whatever, the engine appears to be working well with the 'D1' type remaining on these services until ousted in consequence of heavier trains and the onset of larger engines such as the Billinton 'D3' type.
H.M. Madgwick collection

boiler while Nos 5, *Streatham,* and 18, *Stockwell,* were motor-fitted using compressed air control. (No 27, *Uckfield,* of April 1876, was the first in the class to be motor-fitted, in 1905. For a while she was also oil-fired.)

Six more 'D's appeared in 1877, Nos 292-7, although these and all the others in the class, extant and planned, were re-classified 'D1' upon introduction of the tender version of the class as 'D2' in 1876. This particular batch arrived in haphazard numerical order. Three of them, Nos 295-7, sported Isle of Wight names, although regal No 296, *Osborne,* later found itself downgraded to plebeian *Peckham.* (As the LBSCR was joint owner with the LSWR of the line in Ryde from Pierhead to St John's Road, such naming was justified.) The origins of some of the names might even be said to be confusing. No 293 for example, which carried the name *Norbury,* was likely related to Norbury Park near Dorking rather than the London suburb of that name. All six of the 1877 build were scrapped

by the Southern with only Nos 294 and 297 acquiring the additional 2000 to their numbers post-1931.

In building terms, a hiatus of eighteen months was followed by the introduction of another half-dozen numbered 286-91 in June 1879. These were followed by Nos 280-5 in October and Nos 274-9 in December of the same year. May 1880 saw Nos 269-73 emerge from the works though again, as seemed to be the Brighton's way, not in the order of numbering. With the odd exception these carried names of Wealden locations, including some major estates. Eleven of them lasted long enough to receive the additional SR 2000 to the number after 1931, and of these five, Nos 269, *Crawley,* 274, *Guildford,* 283 *Aldgate,* 286, *Ranmore* and 289, *Holmbury* survived into Nationalisation, although long devoid of any identification other than their numbers. Nos 269, 283 and 289 were also being motor-fitted. As noted earlier, No 268, the lowest numbered of this lot of thirty but the last into service, in June 1880, was the first 'D' to have iron brake blocks.

Another fifteen months elapsed before thirty-four more appeared over the period October 1881 to November 1882. These were built by Neilson and numbered 233-267, although the first numbered was additional to this lot and the last into traffic in March 1883. It contained a half set of motion that had been sent to Neilson as a pattern and thus was known to that doyen of Brighton commentators, Frank Burtt, as 'the pattern engine'. It has been suggested that the delay in delivery may have been because the contract was originally for thirty-four units only and the thirty-fifth was built to a later contract because the pattern happened to be remaining in Neilson's works and the company wanted shot of it!

For these engines we once again find ourselves in Wealden and Downs country with the names, indicative perhaps of the more distant work the class had been undertaking. Only one of these, No 263, *Purley*, did not come into Southern service, withdrawn in 1913 due to frame failure. Most were still at work into the 1930s, half of them receiving the additional post-1931 addition of 2000 to their numbers. Six survived to Nationalisation, all being motor-fitted. They were Nos 234, *Rottingdean*, 235, *Broadwater*, 239, *Patcham*, 240, *Ditchling*, 252, *Buckhurst* and 253, *Selham*.

Brighton recommenced construction in June 1884, although the process was quite drawn out. Two or three engines emerged each month but not necessarily in consecutive months until the last of this lot's twenty-four units came into service in December 1886. Numbers were 221-232, though haphazardly, (231 first, 223 last!), and 351-362, these actually appearing in strict numerical order.

The boilers in these engines had by now also been modified to provide a heating surface of 977 sq ft, a slightly increased grate area of 15½ sq ft and the pressure raised to 150psi. Tractive effort increased accordingly, to 13,400lb. Robert Billinton later provided boilers of similar dimensions, although with the pressure beneficially increased again, to 160psi. Of these No 285, *Holmwood,* was given a steel boiler, the first to receive one. Tractive effort at the usual 85% BP rose to 14,292lb. Names again tended to concentrate on the Sussex coast and countryside, although Surrey got a look in with *Dorking, Coulsdon* and *Riddlesdown*, for example, as did, surprisingly at first glance perhaps, *Kidbrooke*. This is likely to have been named after the Grade II listed Kidbrooke Lodge, near Forest Row in

No 263, the former *Patcham*, and another of the early casualties withdrawn in 1913. Of the 125 built, eighty-four survived to be taken over by the Southern Railway. Seventeen subsequently made it, on paper at least, into British Railways ownership although several of these had been stored out of use for a decade and would never work again. As an example, Nos 2234 and 2274, the former Nos 234 *Rottingdean* and 274 *Guildford* had been out of use at Eastbourne since August 1939 and retained moribund there until towed to Horley for breaking up in February 1950.

Sussex, rather than the locality to be found in the London Borough of Greenwich. As an aside but included to complete the story, the ex-SER Bexleyheath line on which Greenwich's Kidbrooke station stands did not open until May 1895, more than eight years after No 362 emerged from the works. The landowners along the route had for some years been making unsuccessful appeals to the South Eastern to build the line. In the end they formed the 'Bexley Heath Railway Company' in 1885 to take on the project. One of the leading lights and for some time the company chairman, was a Colonel Barne, who had an estate, principally of woodland, to the west of Dartford. The local station he had built for his use became Barnehurst. The company was absorbed by the South Eastern after being declared bankrupt in 1897.

Nine 'D1's were fitted for firefighting in 1940, the pumps being mounted behind the bunker, which required removal of Stroudley's trademark toolbox. They were – by this time – Nos 2215, 2220, 2239, 2244, 2252, 2253, 2255, 2260 and 2357. One of these, No 2244, formerly *Hassocks,* had, post-war, the equipment modified to pump oil during the short-lived Government-sponsored post-war oil-firing scheme. No 2284, *Ashburnham,* was similarly equipped, the two transferring to Service stock as Nos 700s and 701s respectively. All the conversions were returned to normal condition by Nationalisation other than the renumbered No 701s – formerly SR No 2284.

To meet the effects of wartime, seven engines were loaned to the LMS, being posted to Liverpool and Scotland. Indeed, No 36, *New Cross,* by now nameless of course and carrying the number 2699, spent some time working the Lybster Light Railway out of Wick shed, being about as far away from Brighton as one could get in mainland Britain. Some irony too in that a Stroudley engine should find itself at the extremity of the Highland Railway long after its designer had gone south. No 27, *Uckfield,* by then No 627, was condemned by the LMS in 1943 due to firebox damage. The others were back on the Southern by 1944 except for No 2286, which, after return by the LMS, was purloined by the Government for work on the Melbourne and Longmoor Military Railways. It just survived Nationalisation before it was withdrawn in July 1948.

On the subject of boilers, those engines that had not been refitted by Billinton received new Marsh ones. These were of two rings only, with the dome on the second ring, rather larger than either of his predecessors considered necessary and with Ramsbottom safety valves on a manhole over the firebox. The whistle was also re-sited to the front of the cab roof. These boilers carried 170lb pressure, although the heating surface was reduced to 924 sq ft, the grate area being the same as in the Billinton type. Tractive effort rose again, to 15,185lb at 85% BP. The weight also went up, to 43½ tons.

Most of the engines lost their Stroudley chimney in Marsh's time, receiving instead his cast iron one of rather fatter proportions. A few even managed to acquire the heavily lipped Drummond chimney in Southern days. Marsh also fitted coal rails to the bunkers to increase capacity and, at the same time,

as a by-product, reduced Stroudley's carefully planned visibility to the rear. Repainting in umber began in 1905, soon after Marsh's arrival, the names disappearing under the paint and at the behest of the Brighton Board, though No 361, *Upperton,* somehow managed to retain hers for a while. This livery was lined in orange, black and yellow, the whole effecting an estimated cost saving of 45% per engine over Stroudley's ochre with its intricate lining. The Board later relented to permit some engines to retain names, although none of the 'D1's was so redecorated. Those engines that visited the paint shop early usually had 'LB&SCR' inscribed in full on the tank sides, although Marsh later fixed on the simple 'LBSC'. A number of the motor-fitted engines had just 'L&B' writ large and ugly, much to the chairman's disgust. This was soon changed. In Southern days the engines were turned out in lined Maunsell green, which suited them well, with the number and 'Southern' on the tank sides. In Bulleid's time, shaded 'sunshine' lettering identified them. Post-war unlined black prevailed, although 'sunshine' lettering was retained. None apparently received either a BR number, logo or livery.

In view of their numbers it is not surprising they featured in several accidents. In September 1897 for example, No 297 derailed on a curve at the bottom of a dip between Heathfield and Mayfield on the sharply graded Cuckoo Line. Regrettably the driver was killed, although there were no other fatalities despite one of the coach bodies parting company with its frames. (Unlike his engines, Stroudley's coaching stock was generally lightly, even flimsily built. See also *The Cuckoo Line* by Crecy Publications.) A similar derailment affected No 273 in April 1916 on the gradient between Crowborough and Buxted, although there were no deaths here. In both instances the state of the track was called into question. Four years later No 360 got into the street beyond Littlehampton station because a shunter had mixed up the brake hoses with those controlling the push/pull system. It appeared the guard had failed to test the brakes before the movement.

No 248 was extensively damaged in November 1919. Hauling the 7.20pm Victoria–Portsmouth train, she was in collision at Streatham South Junction with 'I3' class 4-4-2T No 24 running light from Eardley Sidings to Battersea. There were forty cases of injury, some serious, but fortunately without fatalities. The 'I3' had mistakenly been signalled towards New Cross but in stopping to have the road corrected lay foul of the junction. The inspecting officer, Colonel Pringle, laid the blame jointly on the driver and the signalman. No 248, the former *Ashurst,* returned to traffic with unique rectangular-topped side tanks specially made for her as well as a Marsh boiler and chimney. Oddly however, Stroudley's condensing pipes were retained, although it is uncertain if they were actually in use. As a matter of interest, this incident showed the work expected from the class at this time. No 248's train consisted of eight bogies, plus a six-wheeled van and a horsebox, a trailing load of around 250 tons gross, perhaps slightly more. And the Brighton's Portsmouth Road was no sinecure with the sharp climbs from Mitcham to Sutton, and in both directions to the high point of the Low Weald just south of Holmwood.

No 627, formerly No 27 *Uckfield*, with the garish and fortunately short-lived large 'L&B' lettering seen coupled between vehicles for motor-train use. Motor-fitted locomotives included the addition of a large air reservoir underneath the bunker, as can be made out here. The location is, of course, near Preston Park.

No 297 *Bonchurch* on its side following the derailment between Heathfield and Mayfield. Damage was mainly superficial and the engine was repaired. It survived in traffic until September 1933 just short of its sixtieth anniversary.

No 254, formerly *Hambledon*, in LBSCR days but this time with what are almost oval buffers. Likely these were an early version of the later standard oval type used by the LMS and BR, the purpose of which was to reduce the risk of buffer lock when on tight radius curves. The additional pipework under the buffer beam indicates the engine is fitted for air-control motor train working. *H.M. Madgwick collection*

This time we see No B634, formerly *Balham*, at Brighton and likely fresh from overhaul. Clearly taken post-1923, the engine had but a short career with its new owners, being withdrawn in November 1926. *H.M. Madgwick collection*

Toward the end of the 1920s the Southern's operators were looking around for suitable engines to relieve the ageing Adams 4-4-2Ts on the Axminster–Lyme Regis branch. The choice fell on the 'D1' tanks, although some modifications were necessary, particularly to reduce weight. To that end Nos 276, 359, 612 and 633 (the two latter engines being among a score or so of the first thirty-six to have 600 added to their numbers in Brighton days to signify transfer to the Duplicate List) had the bunkers cut down and the side tank capacity reduced internally. Even for so small an engine with quite a short wheelbase the curves proved too much, just as they had for the smaller 'Terriers', Nos 46 and 68, which Dugald Drummond had purchased for the same duties in 1903. *(A photograph of the bunker end of the cut-down No 612 appears as Fig 11 in* Part 2 of Locomotives of the LBSCR, *published by the RCTS.)*

While on movement to the Duplicate List it should be noted Marsh in particular renumbered many of the engines in the early lot of thirty-six. No 18, *Stockwell,* for example became No 78 in February 1907, had an 'A' suffix added in November 1909 – a first indication of Duplication – then No 348 in March 1913 under Billinton the younger, and finally No 215 in August 1920. The Southern added the post-1931 '2000', old No 18 then being among the last withdrawn as No 2215 in February 1950, a few months short of its seventy-fifth birthday. (I do wonder though, like 'Trigger's broom', how much of the original actually remained?) Few others were renumbered pre-Grouping, although the first three of the 1886 lot, Nos 351-353 became 218-220 at the end of 1920. And as to name

changes *à la Osborne,* No 272, *Nevill* – possibly from that area of Lewes – became *Goring* in August 1897 and No 294, *Rosebery,* honoured *Falmer* instead from March that year.

None of the twenty in this final batch lasted very long in British Railways days, only three being in service in 1950. No 2252 – ex 252, *Buckhurst,* a motor-fitted Neilson engine from November 1881 – went in September that year. This was followed in July 1951 by No 2359, formerly *Egmont,* built at Brighton in December 1886, leaving No 701s, formerly No 284, *Ashburnham*, a Brighton engine that came into service in October 1879, as the last of the class to be withdrawn, in December 1951. But this was not the final 'D1' at work. In February 1948 No 2357, *Riddlesdown,* was sold to Lancashire County Council for use on the private 2-mile long railway from Grimsaugh, on the short L&Y and LNWR Joint Preston–Longbridge branch, to the Whittingham Asylum. The hospital railway closed in 1957, the engine being unceremoniously scrapped at the same time. No doubt it was worn out but it is a pity that with the preservation movement already beyond its birth pangs the chance was not provided to at least attempt to save one of Stroudley's real, if unsung, masterpieces.

Stroudley had his foibles, of course, besides preferring pumps to injectors. None of his engines had bogies and he turned out only seven bogie carriages, six Firsts and an Inspection Saloon, and those in 1889, the year of his death. How his locomotive engineering would have progressed had he continued to resist the use of bogies can only be guessed at but it is known that at the time of his death he was planning

No 2359 in departmental use as a mobile boiler washing plant at New Cross. This engine had been one of ten intended to be fitted with fire pumps in the Second World War and to this end had already been equipped with larger side tanks and a full size bunker. (Only nine were in the end converted.) The additional plumbing for its role at New Cross will be noted. It is not sure how long it remained in this role and was later noted at Dover on similar duties. It was destined to be one of the last of the class to be withdrawn in 1951. (No 359 had also been one of those previously cut-down for work on the Lyme Regis branch.)

an enlarged 'Gladstone' with a 2-4-2 wheel arrangement. It is also believed he contemplated developing a 'D1' with the same configuration. As it was, the class first introduced by his successor, Robert Billinton, was the 'D3', a 0-4-4T, and the first Brighton engine with a bogie since Craven's time. One cannot doubt, however, that it was Stroudley and his engines in their glorious livery and finish, epitomised by the 'D's, that made the biggest contribution to the aura that the Brighton somehow attracted to itself during his years and which, in truth, continues to the present.

*For those not too familiar with the livery – and paraphrasing Hamilton Ellis's description – the yellow was in fact a golden ochre, almost an orange ochre, but with a touch of green in it. The borders were a dark olive green, the lining between the two consisting of a thin vermilion line, a broader black one and then a thin white one. The corners were turned in, giving the lining a degree of elegance. Boiler bands were black-edged vermilion and then, outwards towards the yellow, olive green bands edged white. Frames were black outside, vermilion inside: that colour also applied to the motion plates and pumps. Platform angles, buffer castings and the outer parts of the buffer beams were dark red (officially 'claret') while the valance below the running plate was edged yellow and then, going towards the dark red, in black and vermilion. The buffer castings each had two black bands edged vermilion bisected with yellow lines. The vermilion central panel of the buffer beam was surrounded outwards towards the dark red by a white line, a black band, a yellow line, another black band and a vermilion line. The edges were black with an inner vermilion line. The corners of the lining were again neatly turned inwards. Springs and wheels were yellow, the one with black buckles, the other with black bosses. Guard irons and sandpipes were vermilion while the cab roof was white, the cab interior being dark yellow or golden-brown. Coupling rods were vermilion but the bushes were polished, as was all unpainted copper and brass. The name, in capital letters, the first slightly larger than the rest, was in gold leaf blocked left in red on sea green and shaded right in black.

No 2220, originally built as No 353 *Keymer* in January 1886, and one of the batch of nine converted for fire-fighting at Eastleigh in March and April 1941. The actual pump was located at the rear of the bunker and was capable of pumping 1 ton of water per minute in four powerful jets. The hoses at the front were intended to act as suction collecting the supply. According to first-hand observation by D.L. Bradley, the abilities in a fire-fighting role were most impressive for the first ninety seconds, after which the water jets reduced to a gentle trickle. No 2220 was one of those that saw 'active service', being stationed at Nine Elms on the night of 10/11 May 1941 when the shed was badly bombed. Post-war it is unlikely the engine saw any further service as it was condemned in August 1946 without having had its additional equipment removed. Others of the class that saw unusual service were two used for oil pumping and one supplying steam at Brighton Works. (Further information on the activities of the class as 'Fire-Fighting' engines in WW2 will be found in *Southern Way Special No 3 – Wartime Southern*)

Bibliography

Twenty Locomotive Men, C. Hamilton Ellis, Ian Allan Ltd, 1958.

The London, Brighton & South Coast Railway, C. Hamilton Ellis, Ian Allan Ltd, 1960.

Stroudley Locomotives, A Pictorial History, Brian Haresnape, Ian Allan Ltd, 1985.

Locomotives I have Known, J.N. Maskelyne, Percival Marshall, 1959.

Locomotives Illustrated No 159, The Locomotives built at the Southern Railway Works, No 2 – Brighton, Part 1, 1871– 1906, W.A.T. Aves, RAS Publishing, 2005.

London, Brighton & South Coast Railway Album, Klaus Marx and John Minnis, Ian Allan Ltd, 1982.

Bogie Carriages of the London, Brighton & South Coast Railway, David Gould, The Oakwood Press, 1995.

Locomotives of the LBSCR Part 2, D.L. Bradley, RCTS 1972.

A number of websites were also consulted, of which Grace's Guide and the Southern E-Group provided confirmatory information.

Rebuilding Victoria at the Turn of the Nineteenth and Twentieth Century

The former R.C. Riley album archive yields a small collection of views of Victoria (LBSCR of course) around the turn of the century. Unfortunately years of storage have crinkled some of the pages somewhat and in consequence there are some issues with reproduction, but for views now well over 100 years old I think we can make a few allowances.

Personally I am not a great fan of the 'then and now' topic and so have resisted such an approach with what follows. However, for the modern day traveller, or those who recall the Victoria of the BR era, they make for an interesting comparison.

We start with a view of the old station taken on 30 June 1904. This is the façade of the first LBSCR station at Victoria, which had opened in 1860 replacing the former Pimlico terminus, the latter having stood south of the river. To reach the new terminus meant crossing the River Thames, which in turn necessitated a sharp climb/drop either side so as to allow for sufficient headway for shipping. The new (Grosvenor) bridge was 930ft in length and was also the first railway bridge to cross the Thames in the London area. The large building on the right is the Grosvenor Hotel, designed by J.T. Knowles and built by Sir John Kelk. The station was the work of the LBSCR resident engineer Robert Jacomb Hood. (Insert image - small size – No 17B – no caption required). Despite much in the way of ad-hoc additions to the station over the ensuing years associated with ever increasing traffic, the existing facilities were simply outgrown and major rebuilding work commenced in 1892 with the purchase of adjacent property required for the rebuilding. The late Alan A. Jackson's book *London Termini* is the likely best source for a full history of the station. In it he describes the old station as ' … presenting a shabby and unworthy appearance to the arriving passenger'. Construction/rebuilding of the actual station occupied several years and was finally completed in 1908. Under a magnifying glass it is possible to count at least fifteen luggage barrows in a line under the canopy.

With even more porters' barrows on view, this is referred to as the 'New Station' likely soon after completion. The freehold of the original Grosvenor Hotel – the name for which is visible on the same level as the canopy – was purchased by the LBSCR as part of the enlargements. Following redecoration and a 150-room extension incorporated as part of the new frontage, the new/refurbished building was opened under new management on 10 December 1900 having been let to Gordon Hotels Ltd on a fifty-year lease. According to Jackson, the new hotel wing was of nine storeys (although this does not appear to agree with the illustration here). The new wing was 240ft long and 70ft wide, and also set back some 56ft from the ground floor building line of the old hotel. The link between the two is clearly visible. Constructed in red brick with Portland stone dressing, the whole was a confident display of Edwardian (well almost) opulence following a Renaissance style, reminiscent of a Parisian chateau. This theme was also copied within the actual hotel. Jackson further comments in a positive sense on the clock but is critical of the ' … ugly iron and glass canopy supported on iron pillars'. Soon afterwards the names of the principal towns served by the railway were added to the fascia. Today the Grosvenor is a four-star hotel with the building Grade II listed.

The R.C. Riley albums contain five images taken on the same day, Friday, 19 October 1906, at a time when work was at several stages. In this first image we have what is reported as 'No 2 Section Victoria New Station – used for local traffic'. The engine in the distance is not fully identified but may well be a 'D1'. According to Jackson, the original track into the train shed was laid on longitudinal sleepers cushioned on rubber in due deference to landowners in the area. How long this continued for is not reported.

This is followed by 'A General view of No 2 Section … now in use for local traffic', and, of course, a tantalising glimpse inside. As will be clearly (sorry about the deliberate pun) gathered, Sugg incandescent gas lighting was in use.

Here we see the work progressing and a view back towards the entrance; again the hotel is prominent on the left.

Reported as No 3 section of the new station and now seemingly with most of the work complete – certainly at this, the south end. (The SECR lines are to the right.) Mechanical signalling abounds while there is for the present little if any trace of what would become known as the 'Elevated Electric', although this commenced from what were then platforms 1-5 from 1 December 1909.

A bird's eye view of the proceedings with the cab road also visible. The rebuilt LBSCR station would eventually boast nine platform faces with a middle road between Nos 2 and 3, 4 and 5, 6 and 7, and 8 and 9. The middle roads thus allowed trains standing at the north end to overtake a train at the south end and consequently gave rise to some very long platforms (Nos 8 and 9 were curtailed in length due to the siting of the hotel). One disadvantage, of course, was a passenger alighting at the south end of the platform could be faced with a long walk to reach the concourse and station exit. Bisecting the platforms at their midpoint was Eccleston Bridge, while there existed a luggage subway, parcels office and a 'heating chamber for footwarmers'. Access to the District Railway station (opened on 24 December 1868) was via a subway (provided from 12 August 1878) at the north-east end of the station entrance. It should be mentioned that the neighbouring SECR was not to be usurped and it rebuilt its own adjacent station in 1907. (With apologies for the damage to the lower right area of the original print.)

A look at the interior of the old station replete with oil-lit four- and six-wheeled vehicles and what is a horsebox or two and even a couple of milk churns. The original print has suffered slightly but its historic importance certainly warrants inclusion. Whilst the 40ft wide cab road has likely been deliberately cleared for the photographer, no one has been out with a bucket and shovel! As an aside, the positioning of columns in the centre of the roadway was deliberate and designed so that, should a train collide with a column, the entire roof might not collapse.

Opposite top: **Again apologies for the damage but here we have an interior view of No 3 section. Note the partial smoke troughs, gas lighting, suburban stock and main line train for Brighton, the latter hauled by R.J. Billinton 'B4' 4-4-0** *Balmoral* **and complete with a Pullman car.**

Bottom: **Likely taken around the same time, this is 'No 2 Section' and Platforms 8 and 9. Platform 9 was 900 feet in length and was generally used for main line departures. Main arrivals would come in on the opposite side on Platform 1.** *(More information on Victoria and its associated services will be found in the Noodle Books publications* The Southern Railway Victoria Station *and* The Brighton Elevated Electrification.*)*

LBSCR Rolling Stock
Slip-Coaches and an Inspection Saloon

Excluding the Great Western, the LBSCR was one of the main users of the principle of the slip-coach. According to the excellent *LBSCR Carriages Vol 1* by White, Turner and Foulkes (Kestrel Publishing), the company introduced this method of operation in 1858 continuing through Southern days until the last slip working on the SR in April 1932. This same book affords details of some of the methods of workings in early days and is highly recommended to aficionados of this type of operation.

The Southern Railway, in its staff magazine of June 1932, also marked the passing of this type of working with the following script, 'The Last of the "Slip Coaches". Introduction of additional services, the increased weight of trains by reason of improved rolling stock, the change from Westinghouse to vacuum brakes, further extensions of electrification and installation of colour light signalling – these and other changing circumstances have brought about the gradual elimination of slip carriages. One could write several pages about the slipping of carriages on the Central Section, but suffice it to say that the practice was a feature of the LBSCR services for many years; carriages being slipped at the following stations: Arundel, Ashurst, Barnham, East Croydon, Haywards Heath, Horley, Polegate, Preston Park and Sutton. The slipping of carriages at Three Bridges did not commence until 1 October 1927, when the 5.5 pm London Bridge to Eastbourne was withdrawn on Saturdays and its Forest Row portion transferred to the 5.20pm Victoria, the slipping station being changes from Horley to Three Bridges.'

This short text was followed by a group of four small images reproduced here and with the accompanying general caption (top to bottom). 'The accompanying photographs record the last slip carriages run on the Southern Railway, namely the 5.20pm Victoria to Eastbourne on Saturday, 30 April, slipping the Forest Row portion at Three Bridges. The train was drawn by engine No 790 (Driver Porter of Battersea, Guard Waller of New Cross Gate), and the photos show (1) the train shortly after division, (2) the slip portion running into Three Bridges, (3) the slip portion at rest – note the white tail lamp, (4) the slip coaches about to leave Three Bridges for Forest Row hauled by engine No 2512, Driver Medhurst (Three Bridges).' The images were credited to the initial R.J.L..

David Austin has also kindly provided an article on slip-coach working on the SECR, which we intend to include in Issue No 43.

"SLIPPING THE SLIP".

The arrival and departure of the last slipped carriages at Three Bridges—see article.
[Photos. by R. J. Levett, Waterloo.

A recent and unexpected find are these three images that arrived with only the barest details, 'Slip coach/slip coach interior/slip coach end.' (Indeed it was these three views that prompted this short article – Ed.) The view of the coupled vehicles also shows another of the elongated buffers referred to earlier together with what was the slipping hook on the left-hand vehicle. The interior image has the slipping handle in view – unlike GW slip coaches where there was a centre window, the guard here would not be able to observe the actual slip. The third image view – the exterior end view – is perhaps slightly puzzling, perhaps the opposite end of a slip vehicle as there are no end windows and the vehicle has conventional couplings. (With grateful thanks also to Mike King for his usual expertise.)

The *SR Magazine* images. As was often the case, the name of the poor fireman was not reported but equally interesting, there is no mention of the second guard – each portion of the train would of necessity have had their own individual guard.

Above and previous bottom: **Two images of the unique LBSCR Director's saloon built, or more accurately started, in 1914 and given the number 60. This particular car had replaced an earlier Stroudley-built bogie salon of 1889. As can be seen, No 60 was well appointed, although how much use it actually achieved is not certain. So far as the LBSCR was concerned, this was one of only two twelve-wheel saloons ever built by the company, the other was for Royal travel. No 60 was 60ft in length and contained a 26ft dining saloon. There was also a 12ft lounge, kitchen, pantry and a lavatory. Work was curtailed in the First World War but recommenced in 1918 with the interior fitted out at Preston Park in mahogany and satinwood. Perhaps surprisingly for a unique vehicle, it was not originally fitted with a handbrake and instead was semi-permanently attached to a six-wheel brake van. When not in use, the saloon was stabled at Brighton. It subsequently became SR No 291S with olive green replacing the former umber brown and gold lining. At some stage the windows and ends were altered, the former having sliding ventilators to replace the top lights and in 1934 end doors with a reduced form of corridor connection. Some new roof ventilators were also fitted together with a handbrake. It was also relocated to Stewarts Lane. Under BR it was repainted in crimson and cream and then in 1962 in green. Its final change was to be equipped with electric heating until purchased by the Bluebell Railway in 1965. It is currently awaiting restoration.**

The Lines and Stations Dr Beeching Did Not Close
Part 1: 1841-1947

W e start with a definite double entendre although absolutely <u>not</u> in the way such things might have been portrayed in the 'Carry On' films of yesteryear. Instead, the double meaning here is simply a question: are we referring in the title to the lines that remained open after

Seeing its last passengers in July 1848, here is the original terminus at Nine Elms likely some fifty or so years later and arguably resulting in one of the finest entrances to any goods depot anywhere in the land! The station here together with that at Southampton, both designed by William Tite, was located at the opposite ends of what was the original London & Southampton Railway and with the buildings similar at either end. No longer in use for passengers, Nine Elms became the main goods depot for the LSWR and was located hard by the southern shore of the River Thames. (The original loco works and later the famed locomotive depot of the same name stood opposite but on the other side of the main line.) The decades would take their toll and by the time goods ceased to be handled – from around 1964 onwards – the splendour of the past had long gone. Ironic too, its sister structure at Southampton would also lose its status as an operational railway station in 1967. Nine Elms was subsequently demolished to be replaced by non-railway-related buildings. Fortunately though Southampton survives, albeit in a way that is totally unrelated to railway use.

Beeching had his cull, or is it the lines that were closed before 1963? I think the reader will have gathered it is indeed the latter, and in fact more in the way of mileage than BR closed post-1963.

Unfortunately, short of checking every reference set out below for the respective mileage and comparing same in the various periods, (namely: closures pre-1923; closures 1923–1947; closures 1947–1962; post-1963 closures), it is difficult to formulate an exact mileage sum for each. I will admit I tried and failed. There are so many references and sources listing closed lines, often with differing mileages shown, that I regret that I simply ran out of time. So a plea here, if someone would like to take this on as a project, I know we would all be grateful for an accurate representation. The problem also comes when boundary changes, particularly those post-1948, are added into the equation. What we may be certain of is that the official (RCH) report for the state of the railways on 1 January 1923 records a total of 19,585 route miles, of which just 2,185 are ascribed to the Southern Railway. Yet even here there is debate as the sum of the total for the LNER, LMS and GWR added to the SR's 2,185 comes to more than the 19,585 quoted above!

Hence another reason why, to avoid the brickbats, I did not pursue this particular topic further.

Suffice to say, the railways were a business organisation. Their primary operation was the movement of passengers and goods (passengers are deliberately put first when dealing with the Southern) and consequently like any business, economic realities had to be considered. Thus, if part of that business was operating at a loss, then it was investigated and, if deemed appropriate, pruned. Partly the history of this can be traced back to the First World War. Post-war earlier development of the internal combustion engine had seen motor lorries and then charabancs/buses take to the roads, each with greater flexibility for the movement of goods and passengers than the railways could provide. Indeed it must be recalled that there was for many years little regulation so far as operators were concerned, while it was also certainly not just the Southern that was affected: witness the Great Western Railway's own report into its branch lines instituted in 1926 and which in turn resulted in a number of closures. The LNER and LMS behaved in similar fashion.

When seen as a whole, some of the lines described and closed may need some explanation, starting with the early closures. To begin with, closures were usually related to an expansion/extension, examples being where Waterloo and Victoria replaced the previous termini of Nine Elms and Pimlico respectively.

In the next category we have lines and stations (individual stations are deliberately not being dealt with in the narrative) closed in consequence of diversions, examples being Angering to Ford Junction, and Lewes to Southerham Junction. (In all cases where examples are given the reader is referred to the accompanying tables.)

Let us also be clear, railways that had been built were perceived as necessary. Closure was only considered where there was no longer any need or where there was a change of circumstances. Even politics had overtaken a previous requirement. Indeed, between 1896 and 1911 not a single closure is identified as having occurred on the SECR, LBSCR or LSWR. Closures though would resume at the latter date but reach a height, perhaps understandably, in the period 1914–18. There were far more, in fact, during the First World war than occurred during the Second, but against this it must be said the subsequent culling of lines in the 1930s likely saved it from occurring a decade later.

Here we may consider matters as they existed in First World War and for this we need to look at the wider social and countrywide picture then taking place. Men, including railway workers, were being conscripted; as a result operational staff were in short supply and, notwithstanding the influx of women workers to replace those now in France, it made sense to concentrate resources in areas of greatest need. Hence the culling of lines around this time, sometimes admittedly even an excuse for closure, which might previously been considered but not acted upon. Some of those lines closed were physically removed, Basingstoke & Alton for example, other lines such as Greenwick Park were left moribund. The scrap metal drive was

also reaching its peak whilst the physical rails did, or so it appears, also make their way to France or were even reused on new rail-connected facilities at home. With a return to peace, it might well have been expected that lines and trains would be restored, but a public that had managed without had likely now found alternative means of transport and with few exceptions closure was permanent.

Just four closures are noted during the 1920s, two of these in the Thanet area resulting from a long overdue rationalisation of the railways around Margate. The other factor to be considered at this time was the need for the new Southern Railway to establish its priorities and while savings could no doubt have been made, and were indeed likely have been justified in some cases in the 1920s as they were later in the 1930s, priorities were elsewhere, and that one word 'priorities' was simply 'electrification'.

Thus we wait until 1931 for the start of major rationalisation with no fewer than nineteen routes ceasing to operate in the decade. In can hardly have been a coincidence either that often more than one closure was scheduled to take effect from the same day, for it was likely easier to deal with two or more as one.

Just one route, the Elham Valley was closed in the 1940s, and here it would probably be more accurate to say the service was curtailed due to wartime needs – the operation of a rail-mounted gun on part of the branch. Services were restored again in 1947 but would not last long. The only other closure of the decade was in 1948, the East Kent Railway, but this was hardly under the auspices of the newly established Southern Region as the route had only been included into SR jurisdiction from 1 January.

The 1950s witnessed twenty-three route closures (excluding Tidworth, which was only part of the Southern Region due to boundary changes). In total then, the two decades encompassing the 1930s and 1950s may legitimately be said to have resulted in more closures than occurred in later years.

Fast forward and the 1963 Beeching report identified 2,363 stations and 5,000 miles (8,000km) of railway line for closure throughout England, Scotland and Wales. Indeed the name Beeching has passed into folklore as being the man responsible for almost every railway closure at any time. Geographically my own nearest line, the 'Meon Valley' from Alton to Fareham closed in 1955 – and has in 2018 been closed more years than it was open – and yet locally when the topic of the 'old railway' ever comes up, it is still referred to as having been closed by Dr Beeching.

So, as stated, in total the number of lines and their cumulative mileage culled between 1848 and 1963 far exceeded those Beeching was responsible for. Many of the more recent are also especially familiar, Westerham, Bluebell, etc, while others have likely slipped very much into memory to be recalled only once in a while. Let us then venture back, firstly to those we can say for certain that none of readers will personally recall.

Lines closed to prior to 1923:

Eastleigh–Gosport	1841
(Temporary closure due to instability in tunnels north of Fareham, reopened shortly afterwards)	
Nine Elms Junction–Nine Elms (Terminus) to passengers	11 July 1848
(Replaced by an extension of the line from Nine Elms Junction to the new terminus at Waterloo)	
Surrey Canal Junction–Bricklayers Arms	January 1852
Stewarts Lane Junction to Pimlico (Terminus) to passengers	1 August 1860
(Replaced by an extension of the line from Stewarts Lane Junction to the new terminus at Victoria)	
Itchingfield Junction South Fork	1 August 1867
Pouparts Junction–Battersea Pier Junction	1 December 1867
Hamsey–Uckfield Junction	1 October 1868
Havant–Hayling Island	January 1869
(Temporary closure, reopened in August 1869)	
Central Croydon Branch	1 December 1871
(Reopened 1 June 1866)	
Hailsham (old junction)	3 October 1881
Eastbourne (old junction)	3 October 1881
Angmering–Ford Junction	1 January 1887
(Original west coast line)	
Lewes–Southerham Junction	3 October 1889
(Deviation of line out of Lewes)	
Central Croydon Branch (Second closure)	1 September 1890
Hamworthy Junction–Hamworthy (to passengers)	1 July 1896
Waterloo connection (LSWR to SECR link)	1911
Strood–Chatham Central	1 October 1911
Fratton–East Southsea	Aug/Sep 1914
Southampton Town–Royal Pier	September 1914
Queenborough Pier Branch to passengers	November 1914
Gunnersbury–Chiswick Junction to passengers	22 February 1915
Forton Junction (Gosport) to Stokes Bay Pier	1 November 1915
Snow Hill Junction to Holborn Viaduct LL	2 April 1916
Holborn Viaduct LL to Ludgate Hill	1 June 1916
Kensington Addison Road to Studland Road Junction	5 June 1916
Dyke Branch (reopened 26 July 1920)	1 January 1917
Woodside–Selsdon Road	1 January 1917
Basingstoke–Butts Junction (Alton)	1 January 1917
(Reopened 18 August 1924)	
Nunhead–Greenwich Park	1 January 1917
(Subsequent partial reopening)	
Norwood Junction–Spur Junction	1 January 1917
Nunhead–Crystal Palace HL	1 January 1917
(Reopened 1 March 1919)	
Corfe Mullen Junction–Wimborne	12 July 1920

The connection between the LSWR and SECR stations at Waterloo was taken out of use in 1911. It must be debatable how much use it actually had, while no image of a train or vehicle movement over what was a single line has yet been found. Here at Waterloo (LSWR) we have a glimpse of the connection in the form of the covered way above the approach road.

An early casualty in the First World War was the short 1¼ mile branch from Fratton to East Southsea. Opened in 1885 and curiously operated in alternate years by the LSWR and the LBSCR, it ceased operation in the summer of 1914 and would never reopen. Likely the reason for what became a permanent closure was the building of the street tramway system in Portsmouth, part of which is seen under construction here. The location is Goldsmith Avenue bridge and with the image that our good friend Roger Simmonds has been able to tie down as having been taken between 18 March and 30 June 1909. The East Southsea line passes under the road bridge with the expanse of Fratton station and sidings away to the left. The tramway was opened a few weeks after the end of June, the delay necessary to allow the concrete used to set properly. Likely the declaration of war in 1914 was seized upon by the joint owning companies as the excuse needed for closure.

Lines closed 1923 to 1947:

In all cases dates are 'closed from' and mean that the last train would have run the previous day or two days earlier were closure to take effect on a Monday and there being no Sunday service.

Midhurst LSWR terminus	13 July 1925
Ramsgate Harbour Branch	2 July 1926
Ramsgate Town–Margate Sands	2 July 1926
Tooting Junction–Merton Park (via Merton Abbey)	4 March 1929
Canterbury–Whitstable (to passengers)	1 January 1931
Fort Brockhurst–Lee-on-the-Solent (to passengers)	1 January 1931
Hythe–Sandgate	1 April 1931
Gunnersbury–Chiswick (to goods)	24 July 1932
Hurstbourne Junction–Junction (to passengers)	6 July 1931
Basingstoke–Butts Junction (Alton) (to passengers)	12 September 1932
(Section from Bentworth & Lasham to Treloars Siding closed completely)	
Botley–Bishops Waltham (to passengers)	2 January 1933
Kemp Town Branch (to passengers)	2 January 1933
Ruthern Bridge Branch (to passengers)	30 December 1933
(Last train ran on 30 November 1933)	
Longparis–Hurstbourne Junction–Fullerton Junction (to goods) by 29 May 1934	
Dyke branch (to passengers)	1 January 1935
Dyke Branch (to goods)	2 January 1935
Chichester–Midhurst	8 July 1935
Fort Brockhurst–Lee-on-the-Solent (to goods)	30 September 1935
Lynton–Barnstaple Town	30 September 1935
Ringwood–Christchurch	30 September 1935
Basingstoke to Bentworth & Lasham (to goods)	1 June 1936
Note – freight still handled from Basingstoke as far as Thorneycroft's siding	
New Romney Branch (Greatstone deviation)–Dungeness	4 July 1937
Ash Junction–Farnham (via Tongham)	4 July 1937
Elham Valley Line:	
Canterbury Lyminge (passengers)	2 December 1940
Lyminge–Folkestone (passengers) (restored 7 October 1946)	3 May 1943
Lyminge–Folkestone (passengers) service suspended	16 June 1947

Timetable entry – a similar display would feature in many editions for various lines as services were withdrawn, usually for just a single issue following closure.

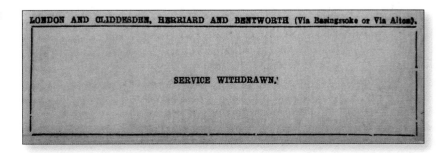

LONDON AND CLIDDESDEN, HERRIARD AND BENTWORTH (Via Basingstoke or Via Alton).

SERVICE WITHDRAWN.

Several lines were closed from 1 January 1917 and not just in the south of England. This was in response to a request by the Government for rails that might be reused elsewhere to assist the war effort. In the case of the Basingstoke & Alton line this was no doubt a welcome request, the route being of little strategic value so far as the system was concerned and costing rather than contributing to railway finance. As likely known, while the LSWR would have preferred the closure here to have been permanent, local opposition was considerable and a forced reopening occurred in 1924, notwithstanding the rails having been lifted in the meantime. Subsequently either those who had campaigned for its restoration failed to use it or more likely simply lost interest. Furthermore, with even less trade than had existed previously, it succumbed again to what would this time be permanent closure in 1932, leaving just stubs at either end. We see here the headshunt at the southern end – once the main running line to Basingstoke – that served Lord Treloar's Hospital near Alton with coal and other supplies until the 1960s. *Stephenson Locomotive Society/S.C. Nash*

Opposite top: **Goods shunting at Whitstable Harbour, 13 May 1950. SECR 'R1' No 1339. This line lost its passenger service in 1931, although freight would continue for a further twenty years. On the left is the building of the original passenger station. Later BR No 31339, the engine has cut-down fittings for working through the reduced height Tyler Tunnel on the branch. It would survive until June 1958, a working life of sixty-nine years. Freight was officially withdrawn from the branch in 1952 but was reinstated for a few weeks in 1953 to assist in the devastating floods that wreaked havoc in the early part of that year.** *Stephenson Locomotive Society/S.C. Nash*

Bottom: **A branch that was closed in two stages was that between Sandling Junction and Sandgate. Opened in 1874, the original branch terminus at Sandgate was closed in 1931 and the line cut back to the one intermediate stopping place at Hythe. This too succumbed under BR in 1951. In this view we see the original Sandgate terminus with an engine in the process of shunting prior to returning to its train.**

The short branch from Hurstbourne to Fullerton succumbed in 1931; indeed looking at the list of closures for the years 1931 through to 1935 shows that the railways were not immune to the general economic depression of the period. In some respects it is even surprising that this line lasted as long as it did: opened in 1885, its sole purpose was a political attempt to prevent the independent Didcot, Newbury & Southampton progressing beyond Whitchurch. This ploy failed and the LSWR was left with a line through almost barren countryside that had little hope of covering its operating, let alone its construction costs, although it was fortunate that freight traffic from the two intermediate stations at Longparish and Wherwell (the latter pronounced locally as 'Whirll') was to a reasonable degree. However, on its own this was insufficient to prevent economy measures and in consequence the route was singled in 1913, while passenger services, usually in the form of an Andover–Whitchurch–Fullerton shuttle, continued for almost another twenty years. Here Adams 'A12' No 614 stands at Fullerton with the typical loading for the line of just a single coach. Three members of staff would be needed for the train, plus station staff and signalmen en route and an allowance for permanent way and other maintenance/renewals. Even a full complement of passengers – which I think we can safely say was highly unlikely – would not have covered the operating costs.

Another line, or to be exact, a station, with grandiose ideas was Singleton between Midhurst and Chichester. Here there had been two island platforms, a subway and even refreshment rooms, all with the intention of dealing with visitors to nearby Goodwood race course, the whole fed from a single line railway at either end. Although popular for a while, the visiting racegoers came to prefer to use Chichester station even if this involved a road trip to the course, although it is known the station was also well used by King Edward VII visiting nearby West Dean House. After 1910 decline set in and the once proud station could hardly be supported on local traffic alone so closure was inevitable, indeed this is another route where it is surprising it lasted as long as it did. Passenger services ended in July 1935, although the line remained open for freight and was indeed well used in the Second World War with trains of munitions sheltered in the tunnels en route until they were required at Portsmouth dockyard. With a return to peace, through freight working resumed but this was curtailed by a bridge wash-out at Cocking in December 1951. After this, freight was soon cut back to Lavant, the first station out of Chichester, where a healthy trade in sugar beet and later gravel continued to be handled until as late as 1991. (See also *SW16* for an article specific to Singleton station.) *Stephenson Locomotive Society/S.C. Nash*

It was inevitable that some local hardship was caused consequent upon the closure of any railway, although as stated, commercial considerations took precedence. It was rare also for any large outpouring of grief to occur, perhaps the British 'stiff upper lip' prevailed or, more likely, few came to be aware of an impending closure simply because the users were few. An example of this might well be the report of the *Portsmouth Evening News*, which commented that just six men and a dog were the last travellers on the Lee-on-the-Solent branch when the final train left the little terminus on the last day of 1930. One notable exception to this seemingly morose practice was the closure of the Lynton & Barnstaple railway in 1935 – note how on several occasions a number of closures were enacted on the same day. Thousands of words have already been expounded by others far better qualified than the present author relative to the end of the L&B, perhaps the fact that being narrow gauge it was perceived as somewhat 'quaint' helped to feed the news furore, or maybe it was simply a quiet news day. Whatever, aside from the newsworthy event, the following day the people of Lynton awoke to find their means of communication with Barnstaple had been severely curtailed. The alternative bus service along roads hardly better than tracks in places was definitely sub-standard in comparison. Yet then, as has been said before, 'perhaps it is not dead but only sleepeth'. Here we see No 188 *Lew* along what was a wonderfully picturesque railway – the observer is not on the roof but definitely in the nearly field!

Also closing on the same day as the L&B was the short Ringwood to Christchurch railway and its one intermediate stopping place at Hurn. (A private stopping place on the line at Avon Lodge north of Hurn closed on the same day.) In this case the rationale behind the closure was fairly obvious. The line from Ringwood to Christchurch and which was subsequently extended to Bournemouth, had been the first means of reaching Bournemouth from the east, this at a time when the latter location was of far less importance than it later became. Add to this the building of a new line from Brockenhurst to Christchurch and the need to take the tortuous route via Ringwood was redundant. Few tears would have been shed at its closure, although in recent years there has been some discussion over the merits of a tram or similar link from Ringwood south, likely this time to head directly to Bournemouth.

To be continued with the post Nationalisation closures.

Ambulance Trains in War
SE&CR

David Austin

A poor quality but nevertheless extremely rare image of a train on the steeply graded Netley Hospital line. The main hospital tower is in the background with the train making its way up the steep grade towards Netley station and the junction with the Fareham to Southampton railway.
Malcolm Snellgrove collection

The development of the ambulance train really started in the late 1800s as the railways moved from the luxury travel of the wealthy few into the mass transport of commuters, holidaymakers and the merchandise of the Empire. The railway companies were still learning how to run trains safely, so it was not surprising that accidents abounded with fearful regularity. As the companies laid the metals across land that was devoid of human habitation, so the advancing railheads moved further away from medical assistance. The need for ambulances on the rails was embraced by England, America and Germany in the aftermath of serious accidents that were attended by deadly consequences. The railway companies responded by building ambulance carriages supported by medical staff. These early efforts transformed everyday carriages into ambulances equipped for medical care that could be used in rescue trains for their customers.

The railways were also the ultimate instrument of war in the early global conflicts of the twentieth century and, while feeding in more and more soldiers into the front line, provided a means to save the lives of casualties from the battlefields. There was a need for whole trains of ambulance carriages that could carry a range of medical facilities from surgical procedures to nursing the wounded. In the early days of the Great War any railway vehicle that could roll on its wheels was pressed into service. Apart from carrying war horses to the front line, the infamous freight wagons of the French railways transported the wounded back to safety. There were serious shortcomings with this approach as the health of the wounded soldiers deteriorated in the rough riding wagons or from lack of immediate medical care. The early 1900s saw the first purpose-built carriages specifically designed for the conveyance and treatment of the wounded and sick. The ambulance train, with a staff of regular army and volunteer medical specialists, matured into a sophisticated mobile hospital in the latter days of the 1914–18 war. The ambulance train service served with great distinction throughout the Second World War, saving many lives and improving the well-being of the injured and sick soldiers. As a measure of their bravery in the field of battle, on the plains of the Crimea in 1864 to the fall of Berlin in 1945, the number of Victoria Crosses that were awarded to individuals in the medical services was no fewer than thirty-six. This remarkable fact is all the more impressive as these unarmed soldiers attempted to save the lives of their comrades while under enemy fire.

Ambulance Trains 1850 to 1914

The evolution of the railway ambulance started in the mid-1800s when the French army under the leadership of Napoleon III experimented with railway wagons to transport casualties. In 1857, at the annual summer camp at Chalons, the army tried out new techniques for using the electric telegraph for passing orders and for removing the wounded. As the railway transports were emptied of cavalry soldiers and their horses at the front, it was found that the straw on the wagon floor was eminently suitable as mattresses for the wounded and sick. The lettering on the sides of the wagons, *'8 chevaux (en long) 40 hommes',* translated as eight horses or forty men, was to become horribly familiar to the wounded British soldiers in the Great War.

The Crimean War (1854–56) and the Franco–Austrian War of 1859 laid bare some serious inadequacies in the provision of military medical services, but these conflicts were to presage some momentous developments in the ways that wars were to be fought. The earliest recorded history of trains being used as ambulances was in 1854 where, in the Crimean War, a 5ft 3in gauge railway was laid to convey supplies to the front and casualties to the rear. The two steam locomotive used in this work were named *Alliance* and *Victory*. The Crimean War also introduced ambulance transport services into the military, which were manned by troops of the Hospital Conveyance Corps before becoming the Land Transport Corps in 1855. The arrival of Florence Nightingale as an organiser of nurses, and Mary Seacole who administered first aid to troops in the trenches, prompted the creation of the Army Nursing Service.

In the Franco–Prussian conflict, the Battle of Solferino was the trigger for the creation of the Geneva Convention after huge numbers of wounded men died on the battlefield for the lack of care. The large-scale evacuation of patients by railway during the battle was the first organised endeavour to move patients by railway. Over a period of several months the French army liberated the hospitals at nearby Brescia from the enemy Austrian forces and transported 89,000 patients to Milan by train.

LONDON AND SOUTH WESTERN RAILWAY. | INSTRUCTIO__ No. 17, 1900

SOUTHAMPTON AND FAREHAM LINE.

Instructions to District Superintendents, Station Masters, Inspectors, Enginemen, Guards, Signalmen, and all others concerned, as to the

OPENING OF A NEW LINE

BETWEEN

NETLEY STATION

AND THE

ROYAL VICTORIA HOSPITAL,

ON WEDNESDAY, 18th APRIL, 1900.

The New Line to the Royal Victoria Hospital runs out of the Southampton and Fareham Line at the eastern end of Netley Station. It is a Single Line, 48 chains in length, and will be worked under the Pilotman System as described in Appendix II., pages 167, 168 and 169 of the Book of Rules and Regulations. The Pilotman will wear a Red Armlet, and must accompany every Train. Pilotman Tickets will not be used. There is only one Station situated at the Royal Victoria Hospital.

The Line falls from Netley Station to the Royal Victoria Hospital at 1 in 80 for a distance of 5¼ chains, then rises 1 in 80 for a distance of 4¼ chains, falling again 1 in 80 for a length of 12¼ chains, the remainder of the line being level.

The Line will only be opened as required for the running of Special Trains, which will be duly advised.

The official announcement of the opening of the line to Netley Hospital. Although out of context for this article, the full history of this short but nevertheless fascinating railway may be found in John Fairman's work, *Netley Hospital and its Railways*, published by Kingfisher in 1984.

This was a remarkable and unprecedented feat of organisation that was only made possible by the help of local people along the route who supplied food and water to the staff and patients. The Geneva Convention of 1864 was to become an effective legal instrument that gave protection for the medical services of the military. It allowed governments to invest in a system of evacuation for the wounded and sick from the battlefield to safety. A purpose-built ambulance train of road wagons was designed and built by the US military in 1863 and a year later Congress passed legislation for the establishment of an ambulance service for the US army.

However, it was the private railway companies that put a practical railway ambulance into public service. In England the chairman of the London, Dover and Chatham Railway, Mr J.S. Forbes, informed his staff that two carriages had been fitted out as fully equipped ambulances. These were based in Stewarts Lane and Faversham in 1866 and were to be called out with the breakdown train 'in all cases of an accident to a train, [which is] attended by serious bodily injury to any Passenger'.

In 1869 the War Department made a request to the L&SWR to provide a vehicle for the transportation of invalids between the ports of Portsmouth and Southampton to the Royal Victoria

Military Hospital at Netley. The invalids had previously been sent to hospital in the ordinary public service trains but the need to provide berths for stretcher-borne casualties could only be achieved with a purpose-built carriage. The railway converted an old six-wheel Post Office van to provide accommodation for patients lying on stretchers and seating for attendants. A second and similar carriage was supplied in 1885. On the Continent, the Prussian government adopted a standard system of ambulance trains and soon had twenty-one sanitary trains in service during the Second Franco–Prussian war of 1870–71. There was a serious crash in 1889 between Stuttgart and Vaihingen and, as a result, the German railway equipped an ambulance train of four vehicles. This train was based at Wurttemberg and, after a further five trains were added in 1914, they conveyed in excess of 150,000 patients during their existence. In 1870 the War Office ordered a six-wheel invalid carriage from the Metropolitan Railway Carriage & Wagon Company Limited. This carriage was 28ft 6in over the buffers and is identified in drawing number 1936. There are no further details of this ambulance.

The American Civil War of 1861–65 is often cited as the first war of industrial proportions. During this epic conflict, the US Congress legislated for the provision of an ambulance evacuation system for the military and the creation of the ambulance service using horse-drawn wagons. When the volume of casualties from the Gettysburg battle overwhelmed this fledgling organisation, the railways were used to convey the wounded. Freight trains were the order of the day for short trips to hospitals for treatment, although coaches with medical staff and urinals were employed for longer journeys. With the outbreak of peace and a resumption of expansion activities, the railroad companies in North America pushed their tracks towards the wilds of the west. As the railheads were ever further away from centres of population, the availability of medical help become more remote. In 1897 it was reported that 1,693 railroad workers were killed on the tracks and nearly 30,000 others were injured. The National Association of Railroad Surgeons (NARS) was established in 1888 in Chicago by a group of medical doctors, who were keen to develop the new specialism of railway surgeons. Drawing on the experiences of the military in the Civil War, [3]the railway surgeons introduced medical transport to the railroads and to civilian medicine. In the absence of tarmac roads and reliable motor cars, they developed sophisticated and specialised railway vehicles to be dispatched to the site of an injury. The Baltimore & Ohio Southwestern Railroad and the Central Railway of New Jersey introduced the first such 'hospital cars' around 1894, and other railroads quickly followed. One common design provided a holding area for three to four patients and a fully stocked operating room. These cars provided a hospital-quality environment in which the surgeon could stabilise a patient before sending him or her on a long journey to a regular hospital. Such treatment ranged from simple wound cleansing to major surgical procedures.

The L&SWR also responded to a request from the Admiralty in 1899 for an ambulance coach to convey naval invalids from Southampton docks to Haslar Hospital in Gosport. The carriage is described by Gordon Weddell as being 45ft in length, although a report in the British Medical Journal of 1900 gave the length of the carriages as about 55ft long. Weddell states that the end profile was similar to the 47ft 6in Eagle saloon of 1893, L&SWR drawing 225, with the exception that the sides were straight to allow for the installation of the naval cots. The coach carried twelve cots in tiers of three on each side, and seats for twelve sitting patients, arranged as four cots for officers in one compartment, and eight cots in the main ward. There were folding seats for two medical attendants but no treatment facilities. The BMJ piece commented upon the benefits of the Royal Naval cot. It consisted of a flat wood frame of some 7ft in length and 2ft 6in width, covered in canvas with the end having an apex from which the cot was slung from hooks in the ceiling. The exterior of the carriage was of light coloured polished wood and, on the centre panel, displayed the Naval crown over the St John Ambulance badge. The Admiralty provided purpose-built steam launches to transfer naval patients from their ships to the shoreside. These are described as being 72ft long, with a 15ft beam, and having a shallow 3ft draught. This allowed the boats to access the disembarkation pier at Haslar Creek at all states of the tide. The boat had two steam engines each driving a screw, and two launches were constructed by the RN small boat dockyard at Portsmouth. This facility has recently been reinstated as a part of the Portsmouth Historical Dockyard. The ambulance launches, which were intended to replace the small boats of the warships, provided twelve cots in the forward cabin, grouped as four berths for officers and eight for the ratings.

The leap from single railway ambulance carriages to a whole hospital train was the answer for a new type of conflict on a foreign land. The national railway of South Africa ranged over long distances between the centres of population and provided a strategic transport system in the Second Anglo–Boer War of 1899–1902. Trains were used for troop movement, supply, track protection and ambulance evacuation. There were twenty-four hospitals in Natal and six trains were converted in the Durban workshops from coaching stock of the Orange State Railways to handle the transfer of patients between them. Princess Christian, the third daughter of Queen Victoria, supported and funded a fourth train and this was the first railway ambulance to be properly designed to provide medical care by the inclusion of a pharmacy and medical staff to administer medicines and treatment. The vehicles were designed by John (later Sir) Furley to carry 174 stretcher cases and 200 sitting cases. The train consisted of seven bogie coaches of 3ft 6in gauge and 36ft long and 8ft width with a continuous internal passage of 2ft 6in wide. The train was built in the Smethwick works of the BR&CWR and shipped out as flat packs to be reconstituted in Durban. This was the first train to enter Ladysmith, crossing the Tugela River after the relief of the siege, and entering the town on 18 March 1900 to entrain sixty-four patients. The train was presented to the Government in June of 1901 with a request that it should be used for the benefit of the army in South Africa but it was virtually destroyed by the Boers likely in 1900 or 1901. However, at least two of the vehicles were saved to be used in a new ambulance train.

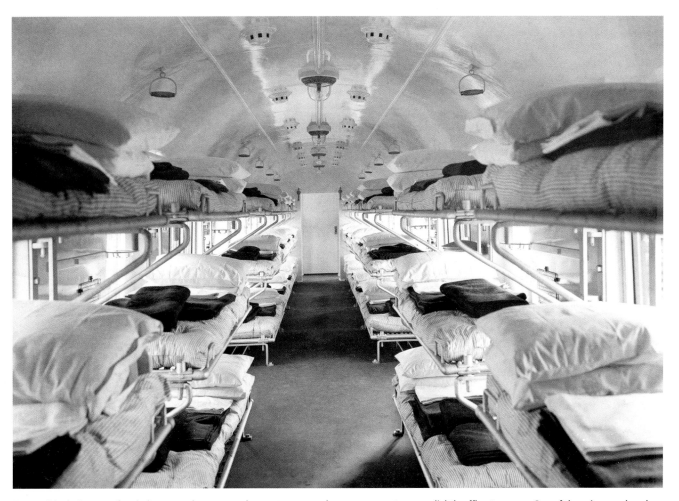

Unsurprisingly, images of ambulance coaches are not the most common, hence recourse to some slightly offbeat sources. One of these is reproduced here and depicts the interior of a GWR ward car of unknown date.

As Ladysmith was being released from the Boer stranglehold, the War Office issued another request to the L&SWR in May of 1900 for a train of vans to be converted to use as ambulances. The five vehicles were 48ft bogie fruit vans to diagram 791, and built in 1900. The train was formally named as the War Department Ambulance Train, and more commonly known as the Netley coaches. The LSWR six-wheel vans from 1885 were added to the train and in the Great War ordinary carriages were included for additional patient accommodation. The train was mainly used for conveyance of officer casualties as the first load off the ships.

In preparing for the First World War it was assumed that the French railways would provide *trains sanitaires* to bring casualties from the front to the Channel ports. Accordingly, the Army Medical Department made provision for just four home and six overseas ambulance trains. The L&NWR was directed to assemble ambulance trains of nine coaches and Sir John Furley was involved in the design of the beds and stretchers for carrying the wounded. However, these trains were not ready for the first major battle of the war so anything on wheels was used to transport the British wounded, including as mentioned the vans bearing the infamous legend from Chalons in 1857, '8 *chevaux (en long) 40 hommes*'.

The anticipation of entering a war was keenly felt by the railway companies. The SE&CR drew up plans for a proposed ambulance train for the Admiralty. The train, of eleven vehicles, was designed to carry 102 cots using bogie brake coaches to provide space for lying cases in the luggage area and sitting cases in the seated compartments. It appears that this train was not built but in the early part of the war the railway did provide two trains of nine non-corridor brake thirds and two brake vans each. These were put together very quickly and were operational in August 1914. In the absence of any photographs of the trains or evidence of medical treatment facilities these were probably used for casualty evacuation from port to hospital. The trains were withdrawn in September and December 1914 when the purpose-designed ambulance trains came into service.

The Great War: 1914-18

In the chaos of a new type of industrial warfare on the Western Front, an unprecedented flood of thousands of casualties was about to overwhelm the medical teams. There were two factors that helped to handle the flow of the bloody wounded. The preparation of the Royal Army Medical Corps (RAMC) for the conflict covered all aspects of a great evacuation system to remove wounded and sick servicemen from the front line to safety and recovery, and a veritable army of volunteer medical staff provided the lifting and caring power to save lives.

In Aldershot at the start of hostilities, on 4 August 1914, a contingent of the RAMC was perfecting the art of running ambulance trains. Six detachments of two officers and forty-five staff (for each of six trains) finished their training and preparation on 12 August. The group embarked at Southampton and, after the crossing, landed at Boulogne. They arrived at Amiens few days later to await their new working offices and homes. It has been assumed that the Continental railway companies were going to be able to provide sufficient rolling stock to form the trains but it was not to be as the passenger carriages and vans were caught up in the war at the front. With the forethought of the well-prepared, the War Office had designed and produced a portable bed frame called the BDA. These iron frames were designed by Brechet, Despres and Amelines to be installed into any type of railway vehicle. Up to three stretchers with casualties could be placed into the apparatus, but although the medical staff on the ambulance trains in France could only report favourably on their use in improvised trains, their colleagues in England favoured a simpler system of wooden trestles. These were designed by Major Leslie to overcome problems with loading the stretchers. However, the early shipment of 600 BDA units was to prove invaluable in the creation of the first improvised ambulance trains in France. The French railways may have been short of passenger stock but the goods wagons were in good supply. And so, on 17 August, at a large junction near Amiens, 100 (non-corridor, as will be explained later) merchandise wagons with a few coaches and passenger vans were handed over to the RAMC group of railway ambulance men.

These were cleaned and divided into three trains with stretcher-carrying apparatus installed into each wagon, so providing beds for twelve lying down cases. During the work to build and to equip the ambulance trains, a temporary solution was implemented to get some of the wounded back to base. The food supply trains left daily for the front and returned as soon as they were unloaded. It was an intelligent thought to load twelve stretcher racks on to one of the goods wagons and, escorted by a medical team, have the empty wagons cleaned out and equipped to carry stretcher cases for the return journey. In this fine example of improvisation, the base received up to thirty-six lying down and eighty sitting cases for treatment. The hard springs of the goods wagons and the lack of inter-carriage gangways were hampering efficient medical care and clearly demonstrated the need for proper medical facilities in the transportation of casualties. It was said that the most popular medical staff were those who were prepared to shuffle along the footboards of a carriage while rattling along the track at speed and to jump across to the next carriage to administer aid to the occupants. Whenever the train stopped, the staff took the opportunity to jump off and then climb back on board to deliver medicines further down

the train. These feats of derring-do favoured those with the longest legs and stoutest hearts.

After much hard work, to the great delight of all the first three fully equipped ambulance trains steamed out towards the front on 26 August. The fourth train followed the others shortly afterwards and, happily for all concerned, the heavy goods wagons were soon replaced with more comfortable passenger carriages and vans by the end of November 1914. The RAMC, under the leadership of Colonel G.A. Moore, was eventually to turn out eleven complete, but improvised, trains of French and Belgian stock. These were fully equipped for the needs of the military and their hard experience of a most unusual war in the fields of northern France was to prove a template for specially designed trains to be built in Britain.

The Railway Executive Council (REC) was responsible to the Government for the management of the railways and had created a number of sub-committees to advise on the provision of ambulance trains at home and abroad. Mr H.S. Dent from the SE&CR was the chairman of the Continental trains committee and, following a visit to France to discuss their requirements, it was recommended that a standard design of ambulance train be created to help the companies to produce trains that could be used by all of the services. The experience of using the improvised trains in operational conditions in France was to become the basis for the standard design. It was determined that four types of ambulance trains were required. The Home Ambulance Trains (HATs) were designed to transfer patients from ships arriving in the south coast ports to reception hospitals in England and Scotland. The Continental Ambulance Trains, (CATs) had a similar role in the war zone but had better medical equipment and were dual braked. The CATs conveyed patients from the battlefield area to the base military hospitals in the rear of the war zone. The Naval Ambulance Trains (NATs) differed slightly from the HAT type by having accommodation for cots rather than stretchers and additional baggage space. The sailors were required to carry their belongings between ships as each ship berth was effectively their home. The cots were preferred by the navy as patients could be moved between the decks of a ship with little disturbance of the patient. The NATs were intended to transfer patients from the Fleet based in Scotland to the hospitals on the south coast of England. The main fleet of the Royal Navy was based in Scotland for the desired showdown with the German Imperial Fleet in the Baltic while, as a legacy of the past wars with England's Continental foes, the three main naval hospitals were located on the south coast to service the main naval bases of Portsmouth, Plymouth and Chatham. The last type of railway ambulance was the Invalid or Unit car. These were single ambulance coaches attached to a normal service train and provided accommodation for a small number of patients. The railway companies of Britain provided thirty ambulance trains for use in France, Egypt and Mesopotamia. The American army in France received another nineteen trains.

The War Office had ordered a set of six Naval Ambulance Trains (NATs) from the London and North Western (LNWR). The trains were actually commissioned as warships and had port

Special working on the Chatham Dockyard branch, 18 May 1959. The train is a special to London Bridge behind C class engines Nos 31721 and 31495, with sister engine No 31720 banking at the rear. The branch joined the main line at Gillingham. *Stephenson Locomotive Society/S.C. Nash*

and starboard sides and day and night watches. Externally the coaches were painted grey with Red Cross emblems on the sides and roof. The navy used cots instead of stretchers to transport patients. The cots measured 5ft 10in long by 2ft 4in wide and there were twenty-four cots per ward car, twelve on each side in two tiers. The day coaches had seating for twenty-eight sitting cases and there were two padded cells at one end of the vehicle. Each train was staffed by two medical officers, and thirty-seven orderlies, cooks and clerks, who lived on the train. NAT 1 was fitted with dual brakes and gas lighting and was delivered to its base at Chatham on 8 August 1914. There are two documented descriptions of this naval ambulance train that bookend the start and ending of the war. These are tabulated below and reflect the development of a common standard for all ambulance trains over the course of the war. The second train, NAT 2, was produced by Wolverton in mid-

1915 and first ran on 22 June 1915. It was based on first NAT but with electric lighting. NAT3 was first run on 2 June 1916 and, as the supply of 45ft clerestory cycle and parcels vans was drying up, the company used 50ft brake vans for some of the ward cars. The next naval train off the works was NAT 4, which was turned out of Wolverton on 9 June 1916 as a seven-vehicle set. This train was to be based in Inverness and there was a maximum load of seven vehicles for a single loco in the highlands. The last train was NAT 5, which first ran on 21 March 1918. By this time the available stock had been used up and NAT 6 was to be a train of new construction vehicles. The train had been ordered in October 1918 and although two cot coaches had been started, the order was cancelled in December soon after the war was concluded. The NATs, with the exception of NAT 4, worked between the Grand Fleet in Scotland and the naval hospitals in southern England on a circular routing, which could mean that patients who had been loaded at Chatham enjoyed a trip to the south-west before routing north to the fleet. There were two trains stabled at Edinburgh, one at Dawsholm in Glasgow, and one, the first NAT 1, was based at Chatham.

In November 1918, Surgeon Commander K.H. Jones, the RN Naval Medical Transport Officer at Chatham, reported in the *British Medical Journal* that the NATs were being used to transport influenza cases. On 29 June 1918 NAT 1 proceeded to Dover from Chatham to entrain 104 cases of influenza for transport to the Royal Naval Hospital, Chatham. The train was at Dover for four hours and seven minutes, during which time the cases were collected from various ships and brought on board. On 10 July NAT 3 proceeded to Dover from Chatham to entrain 140 cases of influenza. The NAT 2 was used on 9 October to convey forty-two Lascars, all with a severe form of influenza, from Gosport to Greenwich. The report emphasised that the medical staff and train crews were protected from infection by regularly gargling with antiseptics and frequent cleaning of the carriages.

These events, notable as the 1918 flu pandemic, were, in fact, two separate periods where the H1N1 avian influenza virus made an appearance for the first time. It eventually infected an estimated 500 million people across the world between January 1918 and December 1920, and resulted in the deaths of between 50 and 100 million people (or 3 to 5% of the world's population). This made it one of the deadliest natural disasters in human history and greatly surpassed the 20 million people who perished in the Great War. In contrast to the usual flu outbreaks (which disproportionately infects and kills the juvenile, the elderly, or already weakened patients), the virus attacked previously healthy young adults. In recent research, using viruses taken from the bodies of frozen victims, it appears that the virus kills through an overreaction of the body's immune system. The strong immune reactions of the young adults ravaged their bodies, whereas the weaker immune systems of children and middle-aged adults resulted in fewer deaths among those groups. The young soldiers of the armies in transit from the battlefields of northern France were billeted in a large staging and hospital camp at Étaples. This was the perfect environment for the spread of the virus, which is thought to have originated in northern China the previous year. The 100,000 Chinese labourers in and around the front line of the Western Front were the most likely carriers of the virus to Europe. The outbreak was called the Spanish flu only because the governments of the combatant countries in Britain, France and the US had sought to maintain the morale of their respective peoples by suppressing news of the pandemic. In neutral Spain there was no need for the censorship, so the perception of a hard-hit country gave rise to the nametag, although in that country the pandemic was called the Naples Soldier.

The Netley coaches, born of ex-LSWR 48ft fruit vans in the Boer War, were called into service again to convey a load of casualties from Southampton on 24 August 1914 to Netley. Princess Christian sponsored the construction of another hospital train for use in France, which was designed along the same principles of the Boer War train. Sir John Furley had built a set of identical coaches of 55ft in length

The Government had enacted legalisation in 1907 to enable the use of skilled volunteers in the medical service. The Voluntary Aid Detachment (VAD) was staffed by members of the British Red Cross Society, St John Ambulance, and Friends Ambulance Unit. This valiant band of helpers was to be on the ambulance trains in France and, in full view of the enemy, performed magnificently in difficult situations. The staff of No 27 Ambulance Train, serving on a train of GWR vehicles donated by the Flour Millers of the UK, was recommended for the Military Medal award in November of 1916. The VAD was the support arm of the army medical services and with properly designed equipment and trained staff, the railway ambulance trains were ready for the next big show.

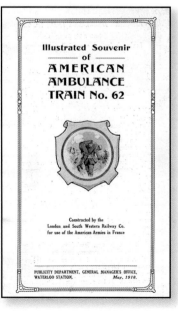

A 1918 LSWR publication. It is not thought that a similar booklet was produced by the SECR. The originals of several of the images from the LSWR booklet may be viewed in Southern Scene, published by Ian Allan in 2008.

AMERICAN AMBULANCE TRAIN No. 62

Constructed by the
London & South Western Railway Company.

THE full story of the War activities of British Railways, under the direction of the Railway Executive Committee, will probably never be told, but since that momentous occasion in August, 1914, when Kitchener's "contemptible" army was so surprisingly transported to France in time to confound Von Kluck's hordes in their march on Paris and the Channel Ports, every pre-war transportation record has been dwarfed into insignificance. Apart, however, from running in this country thousands of special trains with troops, stores and munitions, the Companies have rendered invaluable assistance abroad—rails, sleepers, rolling stock and staff having been sent overseas to provide the necessary railway communications between Base and Front. From the various Railway Works there has flowed a constant stream of munitions, general service wagons, vans, water carts, trolleys, tools, and a number of armoured trains, while in connection with the more humane work of tending the wounded, the railway shops have turned out many complete hospital trains, and thousands of stretchers and Red Cross accessories.

It was, perhaps, inevitable that the South Western Railway Company, from its geographical position, and serving as it does some of the most important British Military and Naval centres, would be called upon to bear a large part of the transportation services. In the reverse direction, to the South

Attendants' Compartment—Infectious Cases Car.

Staff Car—Officers' Mess.

— 2 —

— 3 —

Western has also fallen much of the work of transporting the wounded, and some idea of the scale on which this has been done will be gathered from the recent statement of Brig.-General Hugh W. Drummond, the Company's Chairman, that since the outbreak of hostilities to the end of 1917 no less than 15,500 Ambulance trains, loaded and empty, have passed over the South Western system.

In addition to all this—at their Carriage Works at Eastleigh, the Company have constructed several Ambulance Trains, some for use in Great Britain, others for work overseas.

With the entrance of America into the War, Ambulance Trains for the American Forces became necessary. The American Government, recognising the merits of the British trains, decided that similar stock should be provided for its own troops, and desired them to be constructed by the British Railway Companies, a fine compliment to British design and workmanship.

The latest to be provided is No. 62, completed by the London & South Western Railway Company in April, 1918.

BRIEF DESCRIPTION OF AMBULANCE TRAIN No. 62.

The train is painted khaki-green, with the Red Cross and initials "U.S." figuring prominently on the sides of each vehicle. It consists of 16 vehicles, has a total length of 953 feet, weighs over 440 tons when empty, and accommodates ordinarily 418 persons, or, when bottom beds in wards are converted into seats, a maximum number of 680 patients and staff.

Sick Officers' Car—for Sitting Cases.

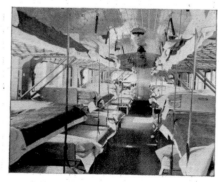

Ward Car—Ready for Lying-down Cases.

— 4 —

— 5 —

Everything that human ingenuity can devise for the safe and comfortable transport of the wounded, and the devoted medical staff who spend many days at a stretch on the train, has been provided. Among the items of special equipment are Westinghouse Brake, Screw Hand Brakes, Passenger Chain Communication, International Screw Couplings, Direct Steam-heating from Engine, Electric Lighting, Electric Fans, Tool Boxes, Fire Extinguishers. The wheels are of special "Steel disc" design, and special footboards and boarding ladders are provided. The important matter of ventilation has likewise received most careful attention.

The plan reproduced on pages 8 and 9 gives a general idea of the accommodation. Commencing from the engine, the first vehicle is the Brake and Infectious Car Numbered A10/6201. The front portion, separated from the remainder by airtight partition, provides working quarters for the railway staff. Access to the hospital section is gained from the platform through folding doors opening directly on to the Attendants' compartment. This arrangement permits the easy carriage of stretchers, there being sufficient room in the Attendants' compartment for them to be easily turned in order to get into or out of the Wards which are situated at either end. In this vehicle are 24 beds allocated to infectious cases.

Staff Car B. No. 6202, providing living accommodation for the medical staff, is next. In the front portion are the dining and sleeping quarters for the sisters, the mess room and bedrooms for the officers being in the rear. The compartments are comfortably furnished with wardrobes, book-shelves, cupboards, tables, chairs, bed-seats, berths, etc., to meet all requirements and a self-contained heating apparatus is fitted for use when steam is not available from the engine.

— 6 —

Ward Car—Ready for Lying and Sitting Cases.

Ward Car—Beds Raised for Cleaning Purposes.

— 7 —

General View of American Ambulance Train No. 62.

BRAKE & INFECTIOUS CAR A10 No 6201

STAFF CAR B No 6202

KITCHEN CAR D1 No 6203

PHARMACY CAR No 6208

WARD CAR A9 No 6213

KITCHEN CAR D2 No 6214

WARD & PERSONNEL CAR C No 6215

BRAKE & STORES CAR E No 6216

Diagram showing arrangement of Eight Principal Cars.

— 8 —

— 9 —

Kitchen Car—Showing Range, etc.

Kitchen Car—Showing Sink, Dresser, etc.

— 10 —

The next vehicle is Kitchen Car D1/6203 containing linen store, pantry and cook's quarters and, centrally, the kitchen itself with large Cooking Range, Soyer Stove and every culinary convenience, with means for quickly heating the large supplies of water required for washing and cleaning. The rear section of this car is utilised for sick Officers able to sit up ; and adjoining is the bathroom equipped for hot and cold water, with shower spray.

Ward Cars (A1/6204, A2/6205, A3/6206, A4/6207) all four of uniform design and arrangement, follow. Each car is fitted with 36 specially designed beds, in tiers of three along each side of the car. When out of use the beds can be folded against the sides of the car so as to facilitate cleaning. The arrangement of the beds can be varied to suit the requirements of the patients. The lower beds may be used as seats, the intermediate beds when lowered form comfortable back rests with the upper beds still available for lying-down cases. The beds can also be used as stretchers if necessary.

Other features in these cars to which attention may be drawn are the central folding door entrance which provides for the easy manipulation of stretchers ; the white enamel surface of the interior, the fixed and portable electric fans (the latter being helpful in "gassed" cases) ; the straps from floor to ceiling to safeguard the patients in transit ; the numbering of the cots and wards as in an ordinary hospital ; folding tables ; portable stools, to facilitate lifting patients into the top berths ; ash trays for smokers ; letter and paper racks ; the provision of blinds to all windows as well as the complete arrangements for controlling the electric lights with which the train is fitted throughout.

The Pharmacy Car F/6208 is the next vehicle. The first portion of this car can be used as a Ward

— 11 —

Pharmacy Compartment.

Stores Car.

— 12 —

for 12 special "bed cases" if necessary, or as an emergency waiting room for men needing medical attention. The Pharmacy occupies a central position and is replete with cupboards, folding table, shelves, water-heater, sterilizing apparatus and sink with ample water supply. The vehicle also comprises a fully-furnished office, emergency room, store for medical comforts, etc.

Following the Pharmacy Car are five other Ward Cars numbered A5/6209, A6/6210, A7/6211, A8/6212, A9/6213, of similar design to the four previously mentioned.

Next is the Kitchen and Mess Room Car D2/6214. The Kitchen is excellently equipped with stoves and cooking accessories. Beyond the kitchen are the Mess Rooms for the Orderlies and N.C.O.'s.

Personnel Car C/6215 follows. This car is of similar design to a Ward Car except that accommodation is provided for the men's kit. It usually accommodates 33 Orderlies.

Brake and Stores Car No. E/6216, the last vehicle, provides for the storing of linen, general stores, kits and provisions and special compartment for meat storage. The extreme end forms quarters for the trainmen.

It will be observed that the numbering of each car indicates the train to which it belongs, and its order in that train. For example, the first vehicle is No. 6201, indicating train 62, first coach. The kitchen and mess room is No. 6214, indicating that it is the 14th vehicle of train 62. By this method, should any of the vehicles be detached for repairs or any other purpose, it can readily be restored to its proper position on its own train.

— 13 —

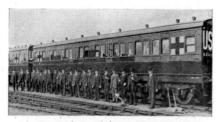

Principal Staff and Foremen at Eastleigh Works.

Right heartily have the Carriage and Wagon Department Staff of the South Western Railway worked to quickly complete this train to send overseas for the alleviation of the suffering of the wounded men of our American Ally, and every individual who has contributed towards its speedy construction may be congratulated on the result.

An ancient proverb states "A three-fold cord is not easily broken," and in this unique triple alliance of a British-made Train conveying American Troops through French Territory we have not only the evidence of the close ties now existing between the three great nations represented by the Union Jack, Stars and Stripes and Tricolour, but a happy augury of unbroken friendship in the future.

— 14 —

COMPOSITION OF TRAIN No. 62

No. of Car	Medical Designation	Description	Accommodation for
6201	A 10	Brake Van with 4 Infectious Wards	1 Train Guard. 24 Infectious lying-down cases
6202	B.	Staff Car	3 Medical Officers 3 Nurses
6203	D 1.	Kitchen Car, with sitting room for sick officers ...	3 Cooks 12 Officers (sitting)
6204	A 1.		
6205	A 2.	Ward Cars, each 36 berths ...	144 lying-down cases
6206	A 3.		
6207	A 4.		
6208	F.	Pharmacy Car ...	12 lying-down serious cases
6209	A 5.		
6210	A 6.		
6211	A 7.	Ward Cars, each 36 berths ...	180 lying-down cases
6212	A 8.		
6213	A 9.		
6214	D 2.	Kitchen Car, with 2 Mess Rooms	2 N'n-Com. Offic'r
6215	C.	Personnel Car ...	33 Orderlies
6216	E.	Brake and Stores Car	1 Train Guard
Sixteen Cars with accommodation for ...			418 Persons, or with a maximum of sitting-up cases a total of 680

— 15 —

— 16 —

Of the Company's employees some 3,000 are members of the London and South Western Railway Centre of St. John Ambulance Association, and besides rendering First Aid to the staff and passengers, also volunteer for Hospital Duty, and, when required, assist in the loading and unloading of Ambulance Trains.

Some members of the South Western Ambulance Centre (London Staff) who also belong to the Surrey County V.A.D. No. 4 Section of the British Red Cross Society.

Opposite and oveleaf: **Second World War Ambulance trains. One at least may be the interior of an LNER vehicle but otherwise details are not known.** *Corbis Images*

World War 2: 1939-44

The rearmament for the Second World War started in 1935 and the intended use of ambulance trains has similarities with the previous conflict. The post-war years had seen the development of the aeroplane into a potent offensive fighting force. The development of the bomber as an effective instrument of war presaged the massive destruction of cities and industrial areas from the air. The Casualty Evacuation Train (CET) was designed to be used to transfer civilian patients from hospitals in London and the south coast in anticipation of air raids. The intention was to evacuate patients from hospitals in the inner cities so that beds could be made available for the victims of air raids. The CET vehicles were not equipped for the medical treatment of patients. Other evacuations were planned from the hospitals within the coastal strip from the Wash to Bournemouth in the event of an invasion. The CET trains were used in the first evacuation of patients in late 1939 and the London hospitals were partially cleared, taking 14,600 patients in all to safety. However, by October of 1940 the predicted bomber offensive on English cities and the feared invasion were becoming less likely. The trains were therefore re-assigned to the military ambulance role or returned to service. The vengeance rocket attacks in July 1944 prompted another evacuation and 13,200 patients were evacuated in sixty-eight train journeys. Eventually the CET trains carried 224,000 civilian and service patients.

The military Home Ambulance Trains (HAT) had basic medical treatment capabilities and were designed for the long-distance transfer of wounded and sick servicemen to base hospitals from the south coast ports. The patients had been brought in by ship from the war zones on the European and Asian continents. The military Overseas Ambulance Train (OAT) was the overseas equivalent of the HAT and was used on the Continent for the transfer of service casualties from the army Casualty Clearing Stations on the front line to base hospitals or to a port. The trains were capable of minor surgical operations and working on Continental railways over very long distances. The last type of railway ambulance was the Invalid or Unit car. These were single ambulance coaches attached to a normal service train and provided accommodation for a small number of patients. The Naval Ambulance Trains from the First World War were not needed in this conflict and the navy used the military HAT and CET trains for the conveyance of their casualties.

The SE&CR provided three CETs for the Ministry of Health, each with twelve vehicles. The train consist was: birdcage brake corridor composite for stores and the guard, five PLV/GBL bogie vans as ward cars with thirty-six stretchers each, nondescript third as a staff car, L&SWR kitchen third as the dining car, a further five ward cars and another birdcage brake corridor composite. At the conclusion of the Battle of Britain in late 1940 and the resulting postponement of the planned invasion of the south coast by the German army, the need for the CETs was reduced and the vehicles were returned to service or transferred to the OAT. The stretcher ward cars of CET 33 were reused in OAT47.

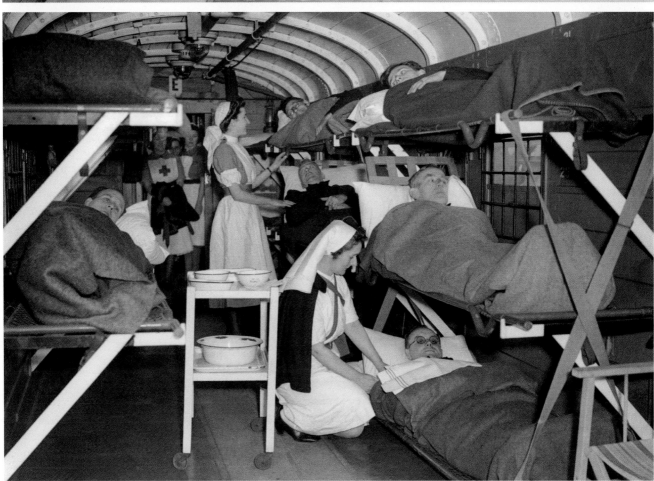

During my research there have been some memorable and sad notes. The diaries of Mr Arthur Dansey Jones, the Outdoor Superintendent of the SE&CR in the First World War, were copied by the SECR Society. He was awarded the OBE in 1918 for keeping the trains moving, and was noted for working sixteen-hour days. His diary of 1918 recorded the number of ambulance trains on the Dover route. In February 1918 he observed and recorded ten trains, but the frequency dramatically increased in March when more than 300 trains were observed as a result of the German offensive on the Somme. It is not hard to imagine that the consequence of some major battle on the Continent would manifest itself in the home land as a greater number of ambulance trains. On a lighter note, the nursing staff of the ambulance trains had had their fair share of incidents. On one train it was noticed the number of patients being unloaded was one short of the total who had been entrained at the start of the journey. A search of the train was carried out with the full expectation of finding a body. It was a relief to find a patient fast asleep in the luggage rack of a compartment. On another occasion the train staff noticed that a lady patient lying in the lower bunk of a train that was evacuating civilian patients had an open umbrella over her head. When asked about this peculiar habit she replied that the patient in the bunk above was prone to incontinence. There was a quick swap around of patients.

The ambulance trains were a great success in the main conflicts of the twentieth century. In the 1914–18 war the number of casualties conveyed to England was recorded as 2.64 million by the RAMC. This represents 30% of the strength of the British army, which is given as 8.84 million. The port of Dover received half the casualties, and ran 7,781 ambulance trains from the port, whilst another 1.2 million arrived through Southampton, about 2,000 in Folkestone and the remainder through other south coast and northern ports. It is worth noting that by 1945 the efficiency of medical care for the wounded had dramatically improved. From the Great War, where eight out of 100 patients eventually died from their wounds, the losses in the Second World War were reduced to only four in every 100.

There were quite a number of ambulance trains in both conflicts and to give a flavour of the specialisation during the world wars the tables below provide a summary of types and colour schemes, and the vehicles of NAT 1 that were based at Chatham station.

These references were consulted for this article:

- Princess Christian Hospital Train: www.redcross.org.uk/ About us/Who we are/Museum-and-archives/ Historical-factsheets/Boer-wars
- The destruction of the PCHT:
- www.warwickshirerailways.com/misc/ misc_brc%26wc142.htm
- The South African Military History Society; Military History Journal Vol 11 No 1 –June 1998.
- RAMC 523/5t, Reports reference Casualty Evacuation, Wellcome Library.
- Robert S. Gillespie, MD, The Train Doctors; A Brief History of Railway Surgeons, 2006. http://railwaysurgery.org/HistoryShort.htm
- Sue Light, http://scarletfinders.co.uk/index.html, The National Archives, WO95/3989.
- Medical History of Ambulance Train Service, Evacuation of Hospitals, PRO MH76-267.
- Philip Millard, Great War LNWR Ambulance Trains, LNWR Portfolio 11.
- Lt Col John H. Plumridge, *Hospital Ships and Ambulance Trains*, 1975.
- Col G.A. Moore, *The Birth and Early Days of Our Ambulance Trains in France*, 1922.
- Surgeon Cmdr K.H. Jones, RN Chatham, *British Medical Journal*, Nov 23 1918.
- E. A. Pratt, British Railways and the Great War, Article from Stand To! Number 27, 1989.
- J.E. Edmonds Official History, 1916, Vol 1, Article from *Stand To!*, No 27, 1989.
- Ashford Drawing No 4111. April 1914, Proposed Ambulance Train for the Admiralty.
- 1918 Flu Pandemic, Wikipedia,
- https://en.wikipedia.org/wiki/1918_flu_pandemic
- LSWR Carriages Volume 3 and 4, Gordon Weddell.
- *British Medical Journal*, (BMJ) 02 June 1900, Naval AT Carriages, pp 1369/70.
- HMRS drawing number – 20005, War Office, Carriage – 6 Wheel, Invalid Carriage, 10ft/10ft w/b, 28ft 6in o/b.
- Sue Light. Great War Nurses, Life on an Ambulance Train In 1914 by M. Phillips. http://greatwarnurses.blogspot.co.uk/2007/05/life-on-ambulance-train-in-1914.html
- E.A. Pratt, *The Rise of Rail-Power in War and Conquest*.
- Mobile Pharmacies of the Great War, Rob Adamson, *The Pharmaceutical Journal*, December 2005.
- Facts About British Railways In Wartime 1943, The British Railways Press Office.
- Frances A. Lord, *They Fought for the Union*, Bonanza, 1960.
- Unveiling the Dover War Memorial, SE&CR, 28 October 1922.
- Diaries of Arthur Dansey Jones, OBE, SE&CR; SEC Society by Jim Greaves, 2007.
- J.S. Forbes, Extracts from Circulars, 31 December 1871; SEC Society.

Ambulance Trains 1900-19

Train	Era	Description	Colour Scheme
Admiralty coach	1870	Ex six-wheeler Post Office van	Assumed to be warship grey, see note at end.
Netley Coaches	1900	ex LSWR fruit vans	French grey top panels, khaki on the lower panels, picked out in yellow and fine lined in red, internal white enamel. An analysis of a photograph with a LSWR Radial loco, a six-wheel parcels van and Netley coaches in the same train shows that the khaki colour of the coaches is a much lighter shade than the brown of the van and the green of the loco. This could indicate that the shade of khaki is green rather than brown.
PCHT	1900	Purpose-built 36ft coaches – narrow gauge of 3ft 6in	Princess Christian Hospital Train 1: white overall, Red Cross emblems, British Union flag and Red Cross on brackets at the end on the roof in accordance with Geneva Convention.
HT4	1910	White Train, South African Railways stock	All over white, small red crosses
US Ambulance	1914	American Train	Brown with US flags and red crosses.
CAT 1	1914	Continental Ambulance Train (Improvised)	Green; French and Belgian stock.
CAT 2	1914	Continental Ambulance Train (Standard)	Khaki Brown; standard LMS and GWR stock, some SR and LNER.
PCHT	1915	Purpose-built 55ft coaches – standard gauge	Princess Christian Hospital Train 2: khaki brown.
HAT	1916	Home Ambulance Train	Vehicles in the HATs remained the property of the owning company; painted in the liveries of the railway; no red cross markings.
NAT	1917	Naval Ambulance Train	Warship grey; LNWR stock.

Ambulance Trains 1939-45

Train	Era	Description	Colour Scheme
CET	1940	Casualty Evacuation Train	Vehicles in the CETs remained the property of the owning company; painted in the liveries of the railway. The vehicles were identified as CET cars by a 2in wide, 24in long yellow stripe on the end vertical corners of the sides of each vehicle; no red cross markings.
Netley Coaches	1940	Home Ambulance Train	Khaki Green; ex LSWR fruit vans.
HET	1940	Hospital Evacuation Train	Improvised temporary CETs; same livery as CET.
HAT	1941	Home Ambulance Train	Khaki Green: white roof, red cross on white square, centre sides and roof.
OAT1	1942	Overseas Ambulance Train	Khaki Green: white roof, red cross on white square, centre sides and roof.
OAT2	1942	Overseas Ambulance Train US	Olive Drab: grey roof, red cross on white square, centre sides and roof.
Unit	1942	single coaches used in service trains	Khaki green.

NAT 1 Vehicles as built in 1914 and recorded by Col John Plumridge

1	Staff sleeping/ Guard	–	BG	Based at Chatham: D377 full brakes were modified by replacing the 2ft wide doors with doors 1ft wide and filling in the space; this allowed the longer cots to be fitted to the internal sides of the van: sixteen train crew in hammocks, guard.
2	Sitting ward car	–	7 compt	6 sitting case per compt, total 42 patients.
3, 4	Cot Coach	–	parcels	Parcels van, 45ft long, 7ft high to 8ft high in the clerestory: 24 cots; two sliding 4ft 6in doors at each end.
5	Day coach	–	parcels	Parcels van, end – 2 WC, centre – 16 wash basins with fold away tables for dining, end – 2 padded rooms 6ft × 3ft 7in + dressing room.
6, 7, 8	Cot Coach	–	parcels	Parcels van, 45ft long, 7ft high to 8ft high in the clerestory: 2 sliding 4ft 6in doors at each end.
9	Stores Coaches	–	brake 3rd	5 compts + guard; sleeping for cook, sleeping for senior sick berth steward, office, stores, isolation.
10	Kitchen + Dining	–	RF	42ft clerestory, one of Manchester diner pair.
11	Family Saloon	–	Picnic Saloon	3 compts: end – sleeping 2 medical officers, centre – dining, end – sleeping for 2 nurses.
12	Brake Guards van	–	BG	Recorded when train created by Col John Plumridge.

NAT 1 Vehicles when returned to LNWR in 1919, compiled by Philp Millard, LNWR Society

1	Brake/ Stores/ Guard	377	BG	Based at Chatham: D377 full brakes were modified by replacing the 2ft wide doors with doors 1ft wide and filling in the space; this allowed the longer cots to be fitted to the internal sides of the van.
2,3,4	Ward car	415	Parcels	Parcels van, 45ft long, 7ft high to 8ft high in the clerestory: 24 cots.
5	Stores + Kitchen	316	BTK	2 WCs at one end, two padded rooms 6ft by 3ft in, dressing room; central portion was 8 wash basins each side which could be covered to become a dining room for 28 patients.
6,7,8	Ward car	415	Parcels	Parcels van, 45ft long, 7ft high to 8ft high in the clerestory: 24 cots
9	Officers Ward Car	76	Picnic Saloon	1904 to LNWR as picnic saloon: was 1887 WCJS sleeping saloon No 263; 3 compartments, the ends were offices for 2 medical officers and 2 nurses, central sitting area.
10	Officers Dining	33	RF	42ft clerestory, one of Manchester diner pair.
11	Medical Staff Coach	62	Picnic Saloon	1909 altered from family saloon: 2 padded rooms at one end.
12	Stores/Brake	381	BG	Five compartments and guards; lockers for clean soiled linen, utensils, dry stores, offices and isolation ward.
13	Brake van	384	BG	Recorded when train received into works 9 Oct 1919; Philip Millard.

Note – As a matter of detail the 'Naval Coach' of 1870 is extremely likely to have been 'Warship grey'. The fleet didn't go grey until 1902 – prior to that it was black hulls with white upper works and buff funnels and masts. Possibly the colour was varnished teak, at the time still a much-used colour. *With grateful thanks to Alastair Wilson.*

The Lost Archives of Stephen Townroe
Part 7

For the latest instalment in this series we move on to the start of 1943. The inclusion of the first image may seem slightly strange and indeed may mean little to some readers, but I hope others will recognise it as a corroded lead plug. SCT adds few words, 'Corroded firebox lead plug – dropped.' We are not informed as to the locomotive involved but he may have been the one conducting the investigation.

Around March 1943 a mobile canteen was provided for workers at Nine Elms in what looks suspiciously like the goods yard area. Female railway workers are seen toasting their good fortune in the company of Mr Allan Cobb (centre, trilby and light colour mackintosh), the SR Locomotive running superintendent. (An article on Mr Cobb appears in *SW13*).

Right: **This we know was taken at Edenbridge but why the camera should have been pointed at a signal we may only guess. Fine, so a good close-up with the fixed shield to prevent any change of a green light appearing when the arm was 'on'. The fittings are of SECR origin.**

Below and below right: **Sometime between July 1944 and June 1945 an accident involving an electric unit occurred either at or in the vicinity of Effingham Junction. Again we are given no further details and an internet trawl reveals no further information. The two views are of the damaged coaches, the second photograph likely to have been taken inside the car sheds at the junction. In consequence of the lack of detail, Mike King has kindly provided the following notes: 'I cannot trace any record of an incident at Effingham Junction, so I would guess it was a depot shunting accident – most probably while shunting a 'blind-ended' five-coach train (3-SUB + 2-coach trailer unit) around the yard. There were quite a few incidents with these, simply because the rush-hour formation was usually 3-SUB + trailer unit + 3-SUB) with just one 3-set used off-peak, so the rest of the train was shunted out of the way. But, of course, the trailer unit had no driving cab, so the motorman was at the far end of the train, or at best in the intermediate cab with little view of where he was shunting. The first view shows coach No 9074 – a Brighton 54ft nine-compartment trailer third to SR Diagram 723 (later 735 owing to changed buffing gear) and one half of trailer unit No 1082 – this number just being visible on the solebar of the coach. Withdrawal is given as June 1945, so this probably dates the incident. The heavy triangular-shaped beam across the coach end, carrying the jumper cables, shows up well and has withstood the collision rather better than the rest of the coach end. (Its companion coach was LSWR 62ft rebuild 10412, originally a 48ft eight-compartment third but with two extra compartments added on at rebuilding in March 1938. This coach went on to be added to 4-SUB unit 4158, also in 1945, lasting for another ten years in this form, before the underframe gave further service under an EPB coach until, would you believe it, as recently as 1993!) The second vehicle depicts the end of a 3-SUB unit where the motorman's cab has seen a good bashing, but I cannot identify it. Looking through withdrawal dates I can find only two for June 1945, but these were from both ends of a 3-SUB damaged at Caterham, so I think it is doubtful it is this one. Most probably the motor brake end was rebuilt and lasted until the 1950s whereas by 1945 the trailer two-sets were starting to be phased out so any damage, however minor, spelt the end for the unit concerned. I agree with you that the location is likely to be within the sheds at Effingham Junction – it certainly looks like it to me, having been around there a few times. The service through Bookham usually terminated in the platform, being shunted into the depot to await the return working, so there was always shunting going on at the location.'**

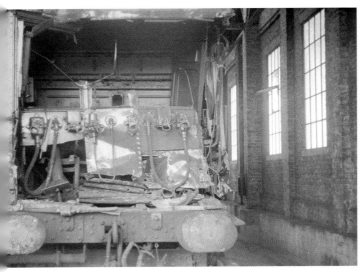

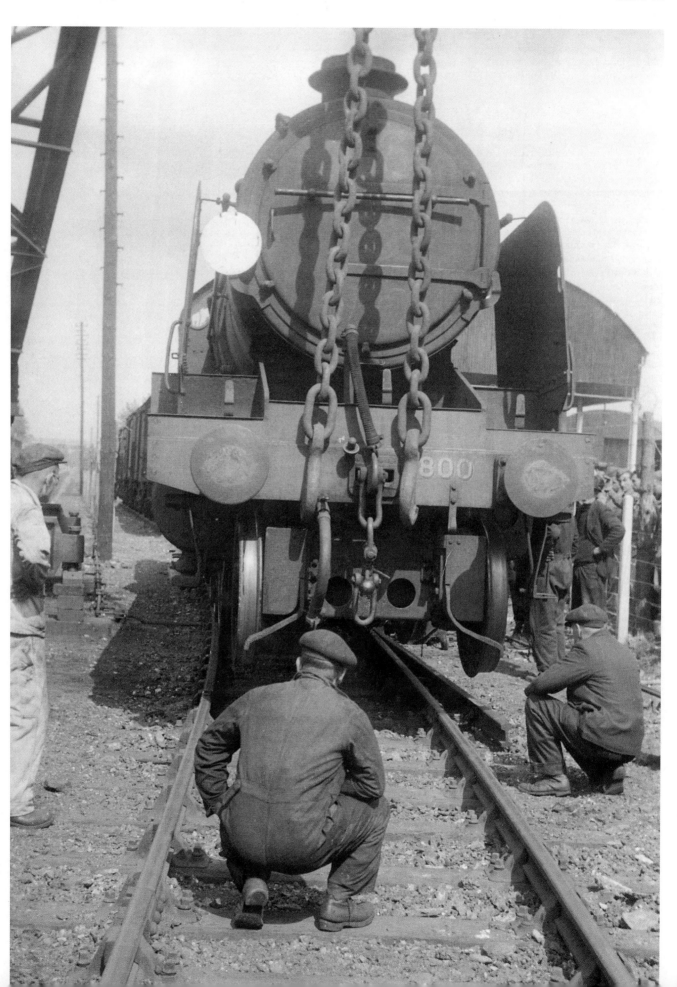

Above and overleaf: **Three views of Guildford shed, again taken close to 'VE' day. Aside from the interest of the engines in view – Nos 270 ('G6' No 270 and likely 0-4-0T *Ironside*) – the other feature of interest has to be the chalk embellishments on the bunker of what could well be another 'G6' – they appear to be rather crude representations of the flags of Great Britain, the Soviet Union and the USA. (*Ironside* was retained at Guildford as the shed pilot engine.) Depot maintenance was also taking place with the turntable being given a lick of new paint.**

Opposite: **What appears to have been a minor incident occurred at Tongham and, according to SCT, 'close to VE Day'. The front end of 'U' class 2-6-0 No 800 from Guildford shed has settled on *Olde England* having come to grief during what appears to be a shunting move. SCT may well have arrived with the breakdown gang as the jib of the crane is just in shot on the extreme left. Certainly the outside edge of the left-hand wheel appears to have experienced some scuffing likely caused by running over the bolts securing the chairs.**

'T9' 119, the Royal engine, in charge of the train conveying King George VI and Queen Elizabeth en route to Portsmouth, where they boarded HMS *Jamaica* for a visit to the newly liberated Channel Islands. The special is seen passing Raynes Park.

A total change now with a portrait image of what appears to be a 4LAV set on a London Bridge to Brighton slow service via the Quarry line. SCT was a keen, and it must be said, capable amateur photographer. This is a fine example of his work.

Off the rails at Farnham with a 25T brake van beyond the buffers and part way down the embankment. Crane No 1561 from Guildford is in attendance. In the three views we see the chains being lowered ready to attach to the frames and, most importantly, the man positioned at the end of the crane during the lift, whose job it was to watch the rear of the crane for the first sign that the wheels were lifting off the track. Should that happen, the lift would be halted immediately to prevent the crane from toppling over.

Another minor incident and not far from that just seen. This occurred at Aldershot in the summer of 1945 and would appear to have been a case of the tender splitting the point blades when running in reverse. The engine is not identified but is likely a member of the '0395' type.

On 31 October 1945, SCT had the privilege of riding on a new 'West Country' No 21C110 (later *Sidmouth*) working between Guildford and Redhill, the engine then just a matter of weeks old. We are not told if this was a trial or an ordinary service working although we do know Driver Honeywell was in charge. (See also p94 of *Southern Way Special No 10* for an image of the engine on the Redhill turntable.

'Watching the trains at Woking'. Mention has already been made of SCT's artistic leanings when it came to photography, well exemplified here. In this short sequence we see two children – not identified – watching, well playing more like, the actual train (not the best image but necessary to include for continuity), and then using the railings and shadows to good effect, the innocence of all being so apparent.

A visit to Eastleigh Works yard with 'Schools' No 911 *Dover* fresh from overhaul and shortly to return to its home depot of Ramsgate. We can likely date this as being around March 1946.

At the opposite end of the spectrum, 'H15' No 334 looks almost as if it is for the chop but it had simply been stripped down for overhaul. The engine spent from February to late June under repair at Eastleigh before returning to its home depot of Salisbury. It would survive a further twelve years in service, being withdrawn and scrapped in the summer of 1958.

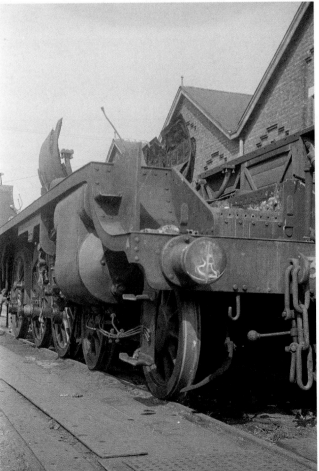

We conclude with a single example of a series taken to show relaying of the up through line at Pirbright with flat-bottom rail. Cranes were in use to lift the section, which likely also explains the presence of SCT. Unfortunately the remaining views of this particular batch are not suitable for reproduction.

***Next time within this feature in* SW43**: *we continue our trawl through the unpublished archives of SCT with a trip behind a 'Merchant Navy', a visit to the Isle of Wight, controlled firing, early 'health and safety', and more accidents.*

Rebuilt
The Letters and Comments Pages

Apropos absolutely nothing (and certainly unrelated to schools train), Roger Simmonds kindly submitted this view of Rowlands Castle station on the 'Portsmouth Direct', reputedly taken c. 1870. If so, this must make it one of the earliest and taken relatively soon after the railway was opened through here on 1 January 1859. The station survives today still with its original building, although nowadays it just deals with passenger traffic, goods facilities having been withdrawn back in July 1961.

School Trains (*SW37*) and Strawberries and Steam (*SW39*)

We start this issue's correspondence with some feedback from the author of both these articles, Richard Simmons. 'The location of the fruit loading times board depicted on page 16 is certainly Swanwick. I was with John Bailey at the time it was taken so have an identical photograph.'

Richard continues: 'So to Roy White's comments in Rebuilt (*SW39*, p.41) that only one down freight travelled over the Broadstone–Hamworthy Junction single line. My description in the Brockenhurst School Trains article related to the situation during the months preceding closure, and I apologise if I did not make this clear. The 5.55am freight from Evercreech Junction–Hamworthy Junction certainly traversed the single line during the time the train operated to Hamworthy Junction, but having trawled through freight Working Timetables (WTTs) in my possession, found it was for a relatively short period of time. The starting time varied between 5.55am and 6am and I first came across the train in the June 1955 WTT, but from 2 December 1957 it was diverted to Poole, continuing to run there until withdrawal from 28 November 1959. There was, however, a substitute service to Hamworthy Junction from 5 May 1958 when a different train, the 6.35am Evercreech Junction–Poole, was diverted to Hamworthy Junction until 12 June 1961, when the destination reverted to Poole.

'In the opposite direction I came across a 9.45am Hamworthy Junction–Templecombe, which from 16 September 1957 was revised to start at 10.18am. The June 1958 WTT described this train as conveying 'empties to Templecombe' but the service was withdrawn from 28 November 1959. In succeeding years there were numerous alterations until withdrawal of freight services south of Templecombe – including from 14 June 1965 when an unusual 15.03 Poole–Yeovil Junction came on to the scene. All these alterations were doubtless part of the Western Region's cunning plan to squeeze freight off the S&D as a precursor to the long lamented closure.

'Moving on to other matters, you will doubtless recall I suggested an article centred on tomato and banana traffic, but I have had second thoughts on that. A short while ago I received an approach from a fellow Old Southeronian's Association member currently researching the history of Southern Railway/Region TSO/Control offices, seeking information on Southampton operations. I loaned him the draft on the Southampton article in *SW* and when it was returned re-read part of it. From this re-reading I realised that quite a lot of information already included in the article could well be repeated in anything new. With this in mind I would welcome your thoughts as to whether a new article should go ahead.' (*From the feedback we have received on Richard's articles over the years – and there have been several (SW6, 8, 12, etc.), it is an aspect of the railway that has been most popular, so we have indeed spoken to him asking for more! – Ed.*)

The Railway and the Cross-Channel Steamers at Littlehampton (*SW41*)

John Farrant the author of this excellent article reported the gremlins had nibbled away at part of three paragraphs from his piece. Rather than jump around, the three are appended in full.

'This article is a corrected version of John H. Farrant, *Mid-Victorian Littlehampton: the Railway and the Cross-Channel Steamers*, The Littlehampton Papers No 4 (Littlehampton Urban District Council, 1972; published July 1973).

'In 1969, Kim Leslie, the founding secretary of the Sussex Industrial Archaeology Study Group, invited me to edit a journal for the group, the first issue of which appeared as *Sussex Industrial History* in December 1970. As a possible contribution he showed me a photostat of a typescript, still in his possession, 'London to Honfleur, by services of the London, Brighton and South Coast railway' by Harold W. Hart, dated 1961. This had been passed to him, in the mid-1960s, by the secretary of the Littlehampton Natural Science and Archaeological Society, to whom presumably the author had sent it. I considered that much more research was possible, on which I embarked. Unbeknown to me until 2017, it had been published as 'Littlehampton to Honfleur, by London, Brighton & South Coast Railway services', *Journal of the Railway and Canal Historical Society* **8 (1)** (1962), 34–42.

'Abbreviations used in the Notes. *BPP: British Parliamentary Papers. Bradshaw: Bradshaw's general railway and steam navigation guide* (Manchester). *JHC: Journals of the House of Commons. LN: The Littlehampton News, Local Guide, Directory and Visitors' Arrival List*. NSR, 'Navigation and shipping returns', *BPP*, annual. TNA: The National Archives. *WSG: West Sussex Gazette.* WSRO: West Sussex Record Office.

'The principal source of information is the archives of the LBSCR in TNA. Generally specific references for statements about the steamer services are not given if they are derived from the following items: RAIL 414/72–75, minutes of the board of directors, May 1863–Dec. 1870; RAIL 414/124–131, minutes of the traffic committee, Aug. 1867–Nov. 1881; and RAIL 414/192–194, minutes of the Continental Conference between the LBSCR and the Ouest (incomplete) and minutes and notes of LBSCR officers' meetings on cross–Channel services, 1870–98.'

Reference also **p85 of *SW41*** and the view of **'H15' No 332**, Jeff Grayer had previously submitted the below, which somehow got detached 'on the cutting room floor'. Jeff states, 'A bit of a mystery this one No 332 with headboard advertising the virtues of British beer. Clearly a pre-nationalisation image, the headboard featuring the brewery of Strong & Co. of Romsey. Given its proximity this view was probably taken at Salisbury. Behind the bogie tender of No 332 is the watercart tender bearing the legend SOUTHERN 330 attached to another of these Maunsell rebuilds. These two locomotives formerly belonged to the ill-fated Drummond F13 class. Only five were built in 1905, Nos 330-334, but they never lived up to expectations and the last example was withdrawn as early as 1924. It had been anticipated that they would be capable of hauling express passenger services between Salisbury and Exeter but they did not last long on these taxing duties. They were subsequently rebuilt by Maunsell as members of the H15 class. They were notable for having very tall cabs, requiring footplate staff shorter than 6 foot in height to stand on improvised stools to reach some controls. This resulted in those class members with this feature being nicknamed 'Cathedrals'. In the background is a wooden bodied coal truck with SR lettering standing on the track leading to the coaling shute seen in the left background. No 332 was to become No 30332 whilst No 330 became No 30330 the former being withdrawn from Salisbury shed in November 1956 and the latter in May 1957.

'The firm of Strong & Co. was sold to Whitbread in 1969 and brewing ceased in Romsey in 1982. They were of course famous for their rail side advertisement hoardings informing the traveller that they were in the "Strong Country". Any further information on the beer headboard and this publicity campaign would be welcomed.

'There were five subdivisions of the twenty-six-strong H15 class, the first being the original Urie design of 1914. This was followed by a Urie rebuild of a solitary Drummond E14 retaining the original boiler but retubed with a superheater. Maunsell then rebuilt the five Drummond F13s mentioned above in 1924, followed in 1927 by a rebuild of one of the Urie locomotives with an N15 type boiler and smaller firebox. The F13s were of massive proportions, as the above image illustrates, which gave a false impression of their power for in practice they were found to be sorely lacking in performance. After a series of test runs on the Salisbury–Exeter route all five were placed into store at Nine Elms in December 1905, ostensibly because winter loadings on the route were lighter but in reality to allow modifications to be made to reduce coal consumption and enhance performance. Unfortunately these modifications did little to improve matters and arrival at Exeter with heavily clinkered fires with time lost became the norm. The LSWR Locomotive Committee called for a report on performance on the route in August 1906 and subsequently instructed Drummond to remove the F13s from the more important services on the line and to investigate their use on less arduous duties. Roles were found for them on Salisbury–Exeter fast freight services and on Southampton–Eastleigh–Salisbury coal trains. These duties became their mainstay until withdrawal in 1924. However, prior to this in 1917 No 332 was allocated to Eastleigh to work refrigerated meat, fruit, brassica and potato trains to Oxford. No 333 received superheating in 1920 but its performance was not substantially improved by this modification and none of the others were so treated. All five members of the class were transferred into SR ownership at the Grouping even though No 334 had been laid aside as unserviceable in December 1921. No 331 was sidelined in February 1924 but the other three continued in service until the summer of 1924 when they were earmarked for rebuilding. In their short lives they covered less than 450,000 miles each but in their H15 reincarnation they managed a further thirty years plus of useful service. The last of the quintet of these F13 rebuilds to be withdrawn was No 30331 in March 1961.'

The Electric Telegraph (SW39)

This from John Burgess. 'I have been a bit late in getting hold of issue 39 of *Southern Way* and was delighted to read the excellent article by Alan Postlethwaite. The application of the electric telegraph was so essential to the development of a safe railway system, and without it, the expansion of the Victorian railway network would simply not have been possible. In this day and age, so much is taken for granted but in the pioneering days there was no mains electricity, so these early systems relied on low voltage electricity produced from primitive batteries (accumulators), which required regular attention to ensure they were working properly and the development of industrial techniques for producing thousands of miles of copper wire, to name just two. I don't think that the pioneers understood how electricity flowed through conducting media, but they were pragmatic enough to know how to harness it and use it effectively.

'Of the pioneers named in the article, to my mind Charles Vincent Walker was the greatest. We think of the South Eastern Railway as being a ramshackle affair, impoverished by years of damaging rivalry with the London, Chatham and Dover Railway (and it certainly was), yet before any of the other Southern Railway constituent railway companies, the South Eastern Railway under his management was rolling out block system train control using the primitive technology of the age and by the time that the LC&DR came on the scene, virtually the entire network then in use was controlled by the block system, only

possible by installing miles of telegraph wire and setting up telegraph stations every 2 or 3 miles. What an achievement! By contrast, the neighbouring Brighton company was still relying mainly on time interval methods for running its services, which led to the fatal crash at Clayton tunnel in 1861.

'As well as the references quoted in the article, there is an interesting account by Michael Harvey in *Southern Way* 12 (From Redhill 'B' to Three Bridges – via Dorking Town, Merstham and Redhill 'A') which describes a signalman's life in these boxes, most of which had their origins with the SER, where some of Walker's equipment remained in use until the 1960s, and this is well worth another read. As I grew up in Redhill I found this article of particular interest.

'For my own personal interest, I have researched some of the history of the South Eastern line from Tonbridge to Reading, including some of the records of accidents on the line, and one I found particularly interesting was an incident at Reading in 1855. Not only is this very early in the history of this line, it is backed up by a very comprehensive account of the inquiry conducted into the circumstances of the accident, and paints a telling picture of life on the railways in the 1850s. Please feel free to use this if it is of interest *(It is scheduled for SW43 – Ed.)*. I have found one very early image of Reading station as it would have been in the 1850s, which, according to Wikipedia, is in the public domain. It appears to show a Cudworth 2-4-0, possibly a member of the 118 class, standing in what would have been the 1855 station. Wikipedia puts the

Certainly not the type of coupling referred to in Philip Miller's letter below, but nevertheless an interesting image of an 'Experimental Auto-Coupler Wagon' taken by Tony Molyneaux in Southampton Docks on 27 March 1965. With all due respect to Tony, it is perhaps a pity he did not record the look of the coupling itself and of which we can find no reference. Can any reader help perhaps?

date of the photograph at 1865–70. The 118 class were introduced in 1857, continued to be built until 1875, and remained in service until 1905, some of the last being found on the Reading line. You will find several references in the text of the article to Charles Vincent Walker.

'If this effort is of interest, I have also produced an article on two accidents on Gomshall bank in 1892 and 1904, for which I would like to try and source some illustrations." *(Accidents are ever popular, even if from the period invariably reported with not a touch of the macabre. I have to agree finding any illustrations for the 1892 event could be challenging but we did feature three views of the 1904 Gomshall crash in SW Special No 8 on pages 44 and 45 – Ed.)*

Automatic Couplings

From Philip Miller. 'Having just picked up the latest *Southern Way* No 35 from Hylands Books in Melbourne, Victoria, Australia, I wish to respond to Jeremy Clarke re Southern emus equipped with MCB Automatic Couplers (of which Buckeye was but one of many manufacturers).

'To explain the correct process of coupling automatic couplers (at least as it applies to the VR – V/Line Passenger) I shall use the example of an Automatic Coupler-equipped locomotive coupling to a vehicle similarly equipped.

'Before attaching the locomotive to the vehicle, the "shunter" (a person qualified to couple vehicles who may be a called a shunter, guard or driver depending on the period and circumstances) will first check that the waiting vehicle coupling is centred and has the claw of the coupling closed and locked. This is tested by the shunter checking that the vertical locking pin is lowered and trying to open the claw by hand. If locked, the claw will not open.

'After ensuring that the vehicle coupling is centred and locked, the shunter will then ensure the locomotive coupling is centred and the claw is open, and the vertical locking pin is raised.

'The locomotive will then be called back to attach. The observing shunter will hear a distinctive clunk sound as the couplers attach and also observe that the vertical locking pin has fallen into place. After which the shunter will then wave the locomotive forward, which will stretch the couplings and ensure that it is locked. The train will re-divide if the couplings have not locked together.

'The sound of a coupler joining but not locking is slightly different, and the vertical locking pin not dropping completely into place is also indicative of the coupler failing to lock. An experienced shunter will detect either a wrong clunk sound, and/or notice that the vertical locking pin has not fallen or bottomed out sufficiently. Providing the above process is followed, the Automatic coupling will not divide.'

A 'rose'-coloured view, No 30108 (*SW40*)

From Frank Spence. 'Whilst I am open to correction, my memory, based on seeing a reference in a book or journal, suggests the paintings of roses within the zeros of the number

of No 30108 was the work of one of the regular firemen that crewed the 'M7'. This would have been after the locomotive returned from its final visit to Eastleigh Works and may infer the name of the rail tour was inspired by the fireman's artistry. The roses appeared on both sides of the bunker. Those on the opposite side of the bunker to the photograph on page 58 can just be seen in the photographs at Grateley (p54 lower) and Salisbury Tunnel (p55 lower).'

On Locomotives

From Eric Youldon, of course! 'Re *SW40* and deflectors on No E772. The "flimsy" stays were raised high to enable enginemen to walk along the running plate between the deflector and the smokebox. There was no room for a foothold on the outside, as the photo on p8 reveals. Note also that *Sir Percivale* has a six-wheel flat-sided tender of 4,000 gallons capacity. This was attached in June 1928 and removed in May 1930. The replacement was a flat-sided eight-wheeler.

'Page 13: The Nelson in the fine photo is No 857 *Lord Howe*, not No 860 *Lord Hawke*. The latter certainly had a non-standard boiler but only insofar as its barrel was a (pointless) 10in longer.

'Page 33: Photo of No 30837. The six-wheel tender pictured here was attached some years after the S15 was built. The batch of the class E832 to E837 had a somewhat varied tender history. In sequence they had 1; flat-sided eight-wheel, 2; Urie pattern eight-wheel, 3; six-wheel 4,000 gallon. Late in life Nos 30833 and 30837 acquired 'Schools' tenders and No 30835 returned to a Urie pattern. For a short time in the 1930s, No 833 was partnered with a Drummond watercart. *(Here Eric makes reference to the Irwell Press book on the 'H15/S15' type – with which we entirely concur – Ed.)*

'Page 88, 21C1 photo. You suggest this shows *Channel Packet* as built. I'm afraid not by a long way! When this Pacific emerged in early 1941 it had the following details that had changed or disappeared by the time your photograph was taken: there was no footstep on the far side; smoke deflectors had yet to arrive; there was no hood above the smokebox door; the 'Southern' roundel was inverted horseshoe shaped; the 21C1 number plate was higher; the three bottom electric lights were immediately above the buffer beam; there was a low down bulbous casing section each side from the buffer beam to the cylinder.

'Page 92. Photo of No 720. Misprinted as built in 1920 – should be 1897. The class was 'T7'; five more double-singles arrived in 1901 as class 'E10'.'

Permanent Way Trolleys (*SW37*)

Some comments from Mike Green. 'I have only just got to reading *SW37*. In the article on Permanent Way Trolleys, p41, it shows estimated costs of £150 for a Key Box installation at 2 miles from a Controlling Token Point and £15 for each additional mile with the statement that there is no idea on how these costs were arrived at. May I suggest the following: most of the £150 is the cost of the equipment and its installation, with the balance made up of the cost of the supply and fitting of the cables needed. This would be at a fixed cost per mile and I would guess that this is the figure of £15 mentioned. This then gives you the price of £105 for the supply and fitting of the equipment. How does that sound? *(Pretty good to me, thank you – Ed.)*

The Schools class (*SW39*). Also Jim Seddon's series in Nos 36-39, '50 Years on

From Geoff May. 'It's sometimes invidious to single out one article in an excellent issue but I feel motivated to congratulate Jeremy Clarke on a most informative article on the 'Schools' class. I share his high regard for such a magnificently proportioned example of the 4-4-0 wheel arrangement – but at the same time totally agree with you about the smoke deflectors enhancing their appearance whilst the Lemaitre exhaust certainly didn't!

'A small correction that doesn't in any way detract from the wonderful nostalgia evoked by Jim Seddon's four-part series "50 Years On". Re the caption on page 49, the last steam-hauled 06.49 Salisbury–Waterloo on Friday 7 (not 8) July was not hauled by No 73093 but in fact entrusted to No 34052 – an appropriate choice since the engine had spent nearly its entire life based at the Wiltshire depot. I attach direct proof as I photographed it climbing to Porton that very morning. Thanks once again for an excellent magazine.' *(Geoff – thank you. Geoff's comments resulted in a series of emails between us and with the wonderful result that we able to bring to a wider audience not just that image of No 34052 referred to, but the other two as well – Ed.)*

Finally last, but by no means least, from Stuart Hicks, on **School trains', freight loading, Mortehoe, and the Class 74 electro-diesels**, vis-à-vis the new 'Special' issue from Simon Lilley and John Wenyon. 'Southern District School Trains. The following Carriage Working Notices (CWN) entries are copied

The image sent by Geoff May as referred to below. The last steam-hauled 06.49 Salisbury–Waterloo service on Friday, 7 July 1967. The train is photographed on the eastbound climb towards Porton and was also the last Bulleid Pacific departure from Salisbury in revenue earning service. (No 73029 took the 18.38 to Waterloo later the same day.)

The second of Geoff May's images. The final original Bulleid at work, No 34102, formerly *Lapford* approaching Weybridge on Wednesday, 5 July 1967 with the 06.49 ex-Salisbury: the same train we saw previously behind No 34052.

On the same day steam had charge of the 'Bournemouth Belle' for the last time. Here is No 34036 approaching Beaulieu Road with the up service. *Geoff May*

as closely as practicable to the printed format. The headings, printed only on the first page, will not be repeated. On the front cover of the CWN is a note "All passenger stock is corridor type except where otherwise shown."

a) Totton–Eastleigh.		These trains are not in the 1953 WTT, but are in the 20 September 1954 CWN: Totton (Weekdays):			
Train	**Destination**	**Formation**			**Previous Service**
		Time	**From**	**Due**	
am					
8 25 **SX**	Eastleigh	1 third 1 compo. brake	–	Berth	–
SX	Berth	1 compo. brake 1 third	4.18pm	Eastleigh	4 36

'The stock remained at Eastleigh during the day. The same applied in the summer 1955 CWN, dated "Until 26/7 and commencing 6/9", but the trains are not in the WTT for this period! In the summer 1957 CWN these trains are not dated, and formed 2-set (513/4).

b) Brockenhurst.		The relevant entries in the September 1954 CWN follow. These show that trains were strengthened on Mondays to Fridays to cater for school traffic.			
Brockenhurst (Weekdays):					
am					
9 32	Wimborne	2-set	6.40am	Weymouth R.P.	8 50
pm					
4 1 **SX**	Lymington Pier	6-set (338)	8.10am	Lymington Pier	8 41
	P. & P. set	3.35pm		Lymington Pier	3 48
4 8 **SX**	Portsmouth & S.	2 thirds 3-set (770)	8.10am	Christchurch	8 37
4 10	Bournemouth West	P. & P. set	2.35pm	Bournemouth West	3 45
		1 third **SX**	6.40am	Weymouth F.P.	8 50
Southampton Central (Weekdays):					
pm					
3 40	Bournemouth Ctl.	3 thirds **SX** 3-set (770)	2.10pm	Winchester City	2 50

'The 8.10 **SX** Christchurch started ECS from Bournemouth Ctl. Set 338 was berthed overnight and at weekends at Lymington Pier. The 4.1 to Lymington Pier also ran on Saturdays, formed of P&P. set only. The 3.40 from Southampton Ctl. added a van **TThSO** at the rear.

'In the 1955 WTT, the 8.10 Christchurch and 8.10 Lymington Pier are not advertised, and dated to run until 26/7 and from 6/9. When these didn't run, the 4.8 **SX** to Portsmouth & S. started ECS from Bournemouth Ctl.

'In the summer 1955 CWN, the 6.40 Weymouth has a 3-set in place of 2-set, and none of the 3-sets is marked (770). The 3.40 Southampton Ctl. has 1 third less. The 8.10 Lymington Pier is formed 1 third and 5-set: at weekends and outside school

term these were stabled at Brockenhurst, and used for the 3.30 Lymington Pier–Waterloo. Was set 338 not up to standard for a Waterloo service? There appears to be no space for stabling at the Pier for six coaches apart from the run-round loop, which would be used for Waterloo trains on summer Saturdays.

'The summer 1957 CWN workings on the Main Line and Old Road differ only in detail, but the Lymington branch has changed significantly. On school days, a second P. & P. set was attached to the 7.4am Brockenhurst–Lymington Pier, and detached at Town to work back at 8.30am. In the afternoon, air control non-corridor second 1098 was attached to the 4.1pm to the Pier and 4.18pm return.

Abbreviations:

2-set	Compo. bke., third bke.
3-set	Third bke., compo., third bke. The suffix (770) identified one of the workings to which the newest sets, (770-793, 805-821, 858-865) were restricted.
5-set	Third bke., third, compo., third, third bke.
compo.	First & third class. (Third became second in 1956.)
P. & P. set	Pull & Push set
F.P.	Front Portion
R.P.	Rear Portion
CWN	Carriage Working Notice
WTT	Working Timetable

'L&SWR Freight Train Loads in the West of England. (*SW39* pp6-9). The departure times quoted for trains on the North Cornwall and Bude lines establish a maximum time frame of June 1903 (3.15am Okehampton to Wadebridge – is 3.13 a mistake in transcription?) to September 1910 (4.5am Sundays Bude to Halwill).

'Starting at Mortehoe (*SW40* p87), a train advertised to depart Mortehoe for Waterloo (summer Saturdays only) can be traced back to 1946, when it started from Ilfracombe as an empty train, Mortehoe 10.4am. In 1947 this train was Q, i.e. conditional, starting from Ilfracombe: the national coal shortage placed restrictions on the train mileage railways were permitted to advertise. From 1948 departure was at 10am, still empty from Ilfracombe, and this continued up to 1953 while the Southern Railway style of working timetable was still used. From adoption of the BR style in 1954 the Ilfracombe departure was 'not advertised' until 1964, the last year of the Southern Region service pattern.

Class 71/74 – 'Thanks for another interesting publication – I have memories of the Night Ferry coming through Peckham Rye from my student days when halls of residence were in Denmark Hill and the hall shop used the Camberwell Cashmart – in the old ac depot in the wye at Peckham Rye … (this was 1975–78). Also, memories of Class 74 in school days heading the 15.30 Waterloo to Swanage (later Wareham) down through New Malden (bridge at London end of station, now sadly with high parapets).

'Two comments: Top of p71. Fast services were normally 70 minutes to (and from) Southampton, two-minute stop and 28 (so 100 in all) on to Bournemouth. 6 minutes to change motive power (often done in 3) and on to Weymouth. Not sure where 1 hour 46 comes from (although certain SO extra trains were slower). Page 83. The 15.30 ran fast to Southampton and Bournemouth (in usual 100 minute timing) changed locomotives (15 minutes) and then left at 17.25 for all stations to Swanage until that branch closed when it was cut back to Wareham. Not until the full hourly fast service (after the extra 4REPs arrived) did it run to Weymouth.'

Greenwich Park *Revisited*

Roderic Cameron

In *Southern Way* No 36 we took a look at the remains of the Greenwich Park branch through the lens of Edward Wallis as it appeared in 1929. The line had been a casualty of the First World War, having been closed on 1 January 1917, and although unlike some minor routes closed around this time ostensibly for material to be recovered to aid the war effort, much of the branch remained intact, albeit moribund and slowly sinking into decay.

This prompted a letter from Roderic Cameron and shortly after the accompanying illustrations. 'David Wallis' article concerning the Greenwich Park branch brought back some memories. I had some connection with the line inasmuch as we lived next to it between Brockley Lane and Lewisham Road until 1970, and as a teenager I could still trace some of the infrastructure of the abandoned part of the route through the streets of this slightly "off-piste" part of south-east London. Amazingly, in preparation of this piece I tried to do something similar on Google Street View and found that there are still some residual traces today, including bits of bridge parapet at road level – despite all the redevelopment that has taken place since the late 1960s when I last did it on foot. An excellent way to trace the line is via the interactive online maps of Charles

Booth, who carried out detailed poverty maps of London in 1898/9 – these are available at http://booth.lse.ac.uk.

'The Lens of Sutton photograph collection contains a number of images of the line taken a year or so earlier than the Edward Wallis photographs in *SW36*. Many of the former have been published before, notably in the Mitchell & Smith book *Holborn Viaduct to Lewisham* (Middleton Press), but it seems appropriate to show some again here as a follow-up to the previous article. I have also included some of my own, albeit taken on a cheap instamatic camera, which was all I had at the time, to show some of what was left in 1968 around St Johns station.

'David Wallis summarised the key points of the history of the branch. Mitchell & Smith also state that the original intention of the London, Chatham & Dover Railway (LC&DR)

August 1928, looking back up the branch towards Nunhead. The station was just east of the bridge that carried the line (and still does) over the LB&SCR route from London Bridge to Croydon. Beyond the station were goods depots on both sides, including a GNR coal depot on the up side (left). These remained open after passenger services ceased in 1916 and some remained in use until 1970. *Lens of Sutton collection*

Looking in the opposite direction – down physically as well as operationally. The overbridge in the background is for Wickham Road, on which stands the parish church of Brockley, St Peter's, whose substantial tower is prominent. *Lens of Sutton collection*

was to continue to Woolwich Dockyard by tunnelling under Greenwich Park. That surely would have been one of the more ludicrous examples of redundant parallel routes unless it just meant joining the South Eastern Railway (SER) line a short distance beyond the terminus and hoping for running powers. Doubtless the Royal Naval College and the Royal Observatory would also have been very influential objectors. I would only add a story related in the summer 1968 issue of *Trains Illustrated* (this was a short-lived magazine in a format slightly bigger than the A5 version published earlier and with the same name by Ian Allan. The 'TI' referred to existed only from 1967 to 1969). It refers to an incident after closure when a set of coaches berthed at the junction at Nunhead was not securely braked and the whole lot ran away downhill to Greenwich – the rumour was that they were not missed for a fortnight!' (Unaccredited images are by the author.)

This is the original LC&DR Lewisham Road station building at the top of Loampit Hill where it joins what is now called Lewisham Way. At the time of this photograph in summer 1968 it was in use as a scout hut. Mostly since then it has been a second-hand furniture and bric-a-brac shop known as Aladdin's Cave, and in fact still is according to Google Street View.

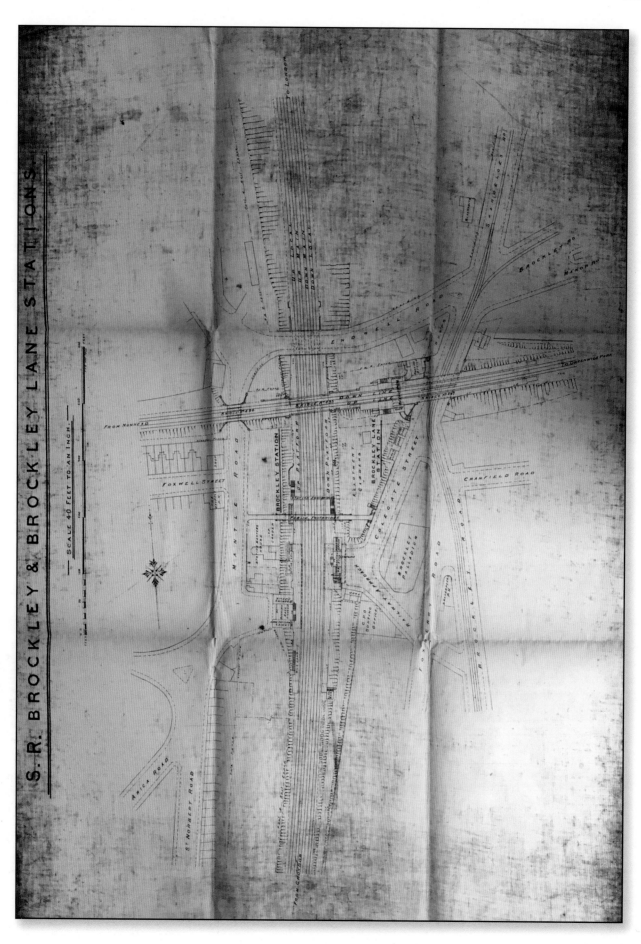

S. R. BROCKLEY & BROCKLEY LANE STATIONS.

SCALE 40 FEET TO AN INCH.

Map of Brockley and Brockley Lane stations, undated (post-1923). *Plan Arch, Waterloo*

Back to 1928, and looking back up the line towards Nunhead. The narrow gauge track set in the up line is presumably related to the demolition and earthworks contractors in preparation for the new loop to Lewisham. Beyond the bridge for Lewisham Way are those carrying the residential Tressillian Road and Breakspears Road. Between 1957 and 1970 I lived in a house on Tressillian Road, just beyond the bridge on the left side. My bedroom overlooked the line and I went to sleep to the sound of 'Q1's and 'W's hammering up the gradient with transfer freights from Hither Green to north London. Later these were replaced by 'Class 33's and '73's. *Lens of Sutton collection*

At this point I should mention that the photograph on page 87 of *SW36* is looking down the line, not up as stated. On that 1929 photograph the steelwork for the bridge over the SER line at St Johns can be seen in the distance. On this image from 1928 the same steelwork can be seen but looking in the up direction with Lewisham Road station in the distance. Shortly afterwards the bridge would be demolished and the line diverted on to the new loop down to Lewisham (to the left), providing a much less congested route for cross-London transfer freight traffic to and from Hither Green compared with the bottlenecks via the Widened Lines, Metropolitan Junction and London Bridge. *Lens of Sutton collection*

The loop to Lewisham as it crosses over the SER main line to Orpington, Tonbridge and beyond (avoiding Lewisham itself). Taken from the 09.40 Charing Cross-Hastings DMU on the down fast line on 17 August 1968, the photograph fortuitously catches a transfer freight heading to Hither Green on the line above. The new loop was available from 7 July 1929, less than two months after the Edward Wallis photographs in *SW36*, so they must have made rapid progress! This, of course, was also the exact spot of the Lewisham train disaster of 4 December 1957, when a Ramsgate express hauled by Bulleid Pacific No 34066 *Spitfire* ran into the rear of a stationary electric train in dense fog. The collision partly demolished the overbridge, and another EMU on the line from Nunhead above only just stopped in time, averting even more carnage. Nevertheless, and tragically, ninety people died. St Johns signal box was at the down end of the station of the same name and on the north side, adjacent to the junction between the Lewisham (slow lines only) and main line SER routes. The original overbridge for the Greenwich Park branch crossed on the side of the signal box, which cannot have helped visibility in the up direction. I am not aware of any photographs that exist of the connection. A temporary bridge was built with the assistance of the Royal Engineers after the 1957 disaster, described in detail by Peter Tatlow in his book *St John's Lewisham 50 years On* (Oakwood Press) – it lasted much longer than the 1929 version and was only recently replaced. The platforms at St Johns had been extended as part of the ten-car scheme in the 1950s. The signal box at the station was closed and demolished in the 1970s at the time of resignalling and construction of the new 'flydown', which enables up trains from Lewisham to use the start of the Nunhead loop to cross over the main line and re-join at the west end of St Johns, thus reducing signalling delays on the junction. Behind the signal box the embankment of the Greenwich Park branch is marked by a line of trees. Peter Tatlow's book refers to the opening of the new loop in 1929 as the point when the rest of the Greenwich Park branch was 'finally statutorily abandoned'.

In 1968 you could gain access to the remains of the old Greenwich Park line embankment immediately north of St Johns (well, as a 14-year old I did!).

In the trees on top of the embankment behind St Johns signal box was this LC&DR milepost, marking 7½ miles from Holborn Viaduct. Unfortunately it was a bit too heavy to 'recover'!

The LC&DR bridge over Brookmill Road (originally Ravensbourne Street), between St Johns and the River Ravensbourne (unfortunately the viewfinder on my cheap camera gave a false impression of the field covered by the lens!). It was still there in 1968, but clearly some of the arch brickwork has been removed to reduce danger to the public from falls. The bridge was demolished shortly afterwards.

Taken from the 1968 *Trains Illustrated* article by Charles Clapper (with apologies for the quality), this is between Lewisham Road and Blackheath Hill where the Greenwich Park branch crossed the valley of the River Ravensbourne on a brick viaduct before burrowing beneath the streets towards Greenwich. This photograph from the early 1960s symbolises the transition between the past and the new housing developments that were transforming the area at that time. Although it only shows one arch here, this is the only image I know that shows the viaduct. Amazingly the railway has now returned to this scene as it is the site of Elverson Road station on the DLR link to Lewisham, which follows the Ravensbourne valley on this stretch. *Credited to Charles Klapper in* Trains Illustrated, autumn 1968.

Back to 1928, Blackheath Hill station is increasingly derelict eleven years after closure, although the down starter signal arm is still there. *Lens of Sutton collection*

Looking back up the line towards Lewisham Road (the station), the Blackheath Hill station platforms extend as far as the overbridge carrying the junction of Lewisham Road (the road) and Sparta Street (originally King Street). The bridge beyond carries Orchard Hill and Morden Street. Today, the site of Blackheath Hill station is marked by what appears to be the remains of the bridge parapet on the eponymous road above. (There is a similar length of wall on the corner of Sparta Street and Lewisham Road.) While it is to the same style as the street overbridges, it looks too new and on the Sparta Street section the alignment doesn't seem quite right. Perhaps they have just been rebuilt in the same style to resemble the originals? *Lens of Sutton collection*

Becoming more like a cut-and-cover underground railway, the tunnel beyond Blackheath Hill takes the line in an almost parallel alignment under Blissett Street as it continues towards the terminus. The civil engineering involved on this last part of the line must have contributed massively to the cost. (Nearing Greenwich itself and 100 years after closure the course of the line, long since in-filled, is still apparent in the area bounded by Royal Hill to the east, Prior Street to the west and Circus Street to the north. The route seems to have been used (at least partly) for allotment gardens. On the north side of Circus Street some old masonry – part of the original bridgework – still survives as wall. *Lens of Sutton collection*

The terminus at Greenwich had three platform faces (it only became Greenwich Park after the operational merger of the LC&DR and SER in 1899 to avoid confusion with the other station of the same name). The two principal platforms shared a central run-round loop, although most regular services were motor-trains. Apart from commuter traffic to the city, day trip excursion traffic was also sought, both for visitors to Greenwich Park itself, and in the opposite direction to the Crystal Palace (reached from the LC&DR's other branch from Nunhead to the elaborate High Level station – a line that closed in 1954 despite being electrified). The canopies provided extensive shelter for waiting passengers. *Lens of Sutton collection*

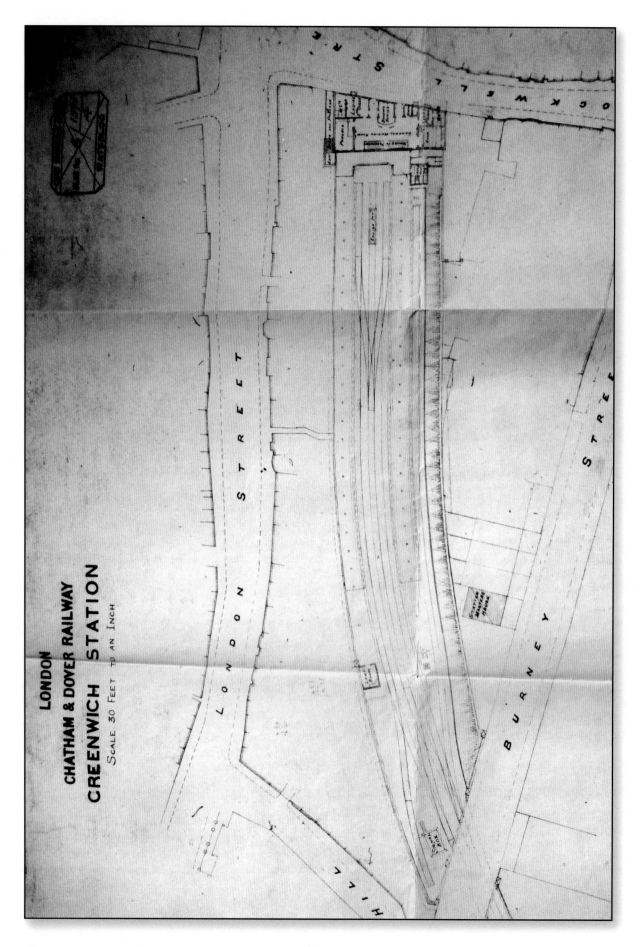

LCDR plan of Greenwich station. *Plan Arch, Waterloo*

If you wanted a prototype for a model of a compact urban terminus, Greenwich Park might make an attractive choice, with scenic breaks neatly provided for by overbridges and elevated Victorian terraced housing. *Lens of Sutton collection*

After closure, the station building was used for many years as a billiards club and later as premises for a building firm. It was only demolished in the 1960s. It is now the site of a hotel, and the station itself is – predictably – a car park. *Lens of Sutton collection*

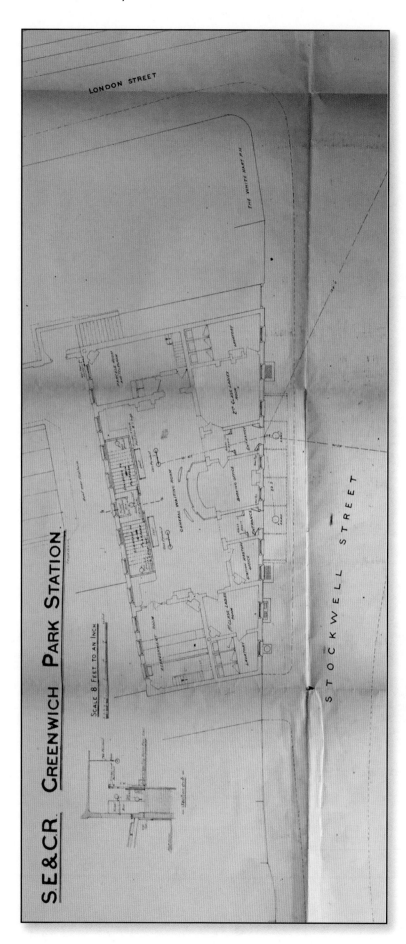

SECR plan of the station accommodation at Greenwich Park. *Plan Arch, Waterloo*

The Horton Hospital Railway

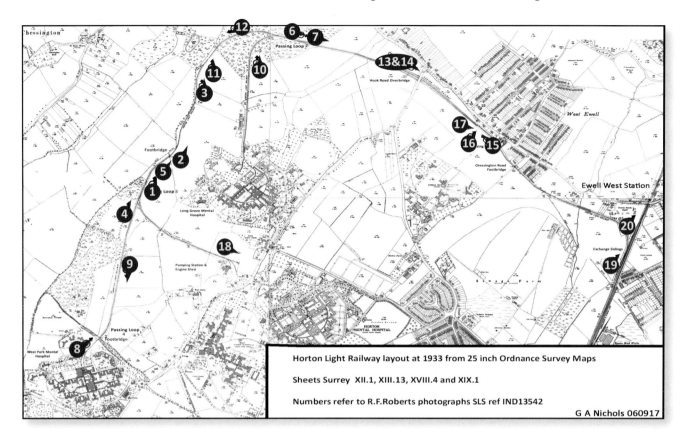

Horton Light Railway layout at 1933 from 25 inch Ordnance Survey Maps

Sheets Surrey XII.1, XIII.13, XVIII.4 and XIX.1

Numbers refer to R.F.Roberts photographs SLS ref IND13542

G A Nichols 060917

mages from the R F Roberts collection, courtesy of the Stephenson Locomotive Society and Librarian Gerry Nichols.

Another follow-up, this time to *SW39* and the piece on the line by John Burgess. Gerry Nichols has identified a number of views on the line within the SLS archive and they are shown here identified by numbered location against the accompanying map:

View 1.

View 2.

View 3.

View 4.

View 5.

View 6.

View 7.

View 8.

View 9.

View 10.

View 11.

View 12.

View 13.

View 14.

View 15.

View 16.

View 17.

View 18.

View 19.

View 20.

Observations at Eastleigh, 19 March 1966

Tony Harris

Editor's note:

In mid-November 2017 I received an unsolicited email from Tony Harris. We had never met but what he sent as attachments to his email interested me straight away as these were images taken exactly at one of the times I had been visiting Eastleigh shed. (The views I took were not to the same standard.) We corresponded further and I am delighted to be able to include some of his images as well as his log of the day in question – the latter especially interesting.

A sad sight outside the front of the shed. The last remains of No 31809, which, together with Standard Class 4 tank 80132, were cut up by contractors outside the front of the shed.

A link with the past. The last 'M7' at Eastleigh, No 30053, which, together with 'Schools' No 30926 *Repton*, alternated locations between the works yard and various roads in the running shed awaiting movement to the Steamtown, Vermont, USA. Both engines were subsequently repatriated back to the UK, the M7 to the Swanage Railway, the 'Schools' to the North Yorkshire Moors Railway.

Date/Day	Location	Class	Number	Details
19-Mar-66				
Saturday	Eastleigh Station/Main Line	MN	35007	Down Passenger – duty 383
	Dull & cloudy damp day	MN	35026	
		MN	35027	Down Passenger – duty 433
		WC	34017	
		WC	34038	Down Goods
		BB	34060	Up Passenger – duty 250
		BB	34066	
		BB/Q1	34089 & 33006	Up Passenger – passing Q1 33006
		WC	34097	
		USA	30067	Light engine
		WC	34104	
		Stnd 5/Q1	73171 & 33006	Down Passenger – passing Q1 33006
		LM 2T	41287	Down goods
		LM 2T	41299	Up Passenger
		Stnd 4T	80083	?
		LM 5	44942	Up Poole–York passenger
		Brush	D1858	Down Pines Express
		Brush	D1910	
		CL 33'	D6503	
		CL 33'	D6505	
		CL 33'	D6516	
		CL 33'	D6536	
		CL 33'	D6549	
		CL 33'	D6585	
		Hymek	D7058	Down Parcels
		D'shtr	D2298	
		D'shtr	D2985	
		D'shtr	D3093	In yard sidings next to station
	Eastleigh Works yard	WC/28XX	34001 & 2818	View from road showing 34001 & 2818
		USA	30067	In steam – works shunter
	Eastleigh MPD – Steam	View		View of rear of shed. Line of dead locos 80142 34048 76019 33020 34008 35023 & 30071 alongside
		MN	35023	Out of steam – rear of shed, coupling rods removed
		MN	35030	In steam – alongside coaling stage

Date/Day	Location	Class	Number	Details
		WC	34008	Out of steam – rear of shed
		WC	34018	Inside shed
		WC	34034	Inside shed
		WC	34037	Inside shed
		WC	34038	In steam – alongside coaling stage
		WC	34041	Out of steam – rear of shed, coupling rods removed
		WC	34044	Inside shed
		WC	34048	Out of steam – rear of shed
		BB	34071	In steam – front of shed yard
		BB	34071	In steam – front of shed yard
		BB/LM2T	34071 & 41287	In steam – front of shed yard
		BB	34079	Out of steam – rear of shed
		BB/Stnd 4	34079 & 73016	Out of steam – rear of shed
		WC	34102	Inside shed
		USA	30064	In steam – alongside coaling stage
		USA	30071	In steam – rear of shed alongside 35023
		USA	30073	In steam – alongside coaling stage
		Q1	33006	In steam – alongside coaling stage + 30064 & 30073
		Q1	33006	Front on view
		Q1	33006	Side view from rear
		Q1	33006	Front on view – leaving depot
		Q1	33020	Out of steam – rear of shed, coupling rods removed
		Q1	33020	Out of steam – rear of shed, coupling rods removed
		Q1	33027	Inside shed
		M7	30053	Outside front end of shed
		M7	30053	Outside front end of shed
		V	30926	Outside front end of shed
		V	30926	Outside front end of shed
		V	30926	Outside front end of shed
		V	30926	Outside front end of shed
		U	31639	In steam – alongside coaling stage
		U	31639	In steam – alongside coaling stage
		U	31809	Behind 80132, coupling rods etc removed

The elusive BR Class 2 tank inside the shed: No 84014. It arrived at Eastleigh with the intention of being cut down for use on the Isle of Wight. (See *SW37*)

A sign of the times. In early 1966 the erstwhile coaling stage was taken out of use and thereafter coaling of locomotives was by crane. The reason for this was that the access road leading to the slope up was required for the extension to the existing diesel depot, and of course diesel would outlive steam. To be fair, the building was in shocking condition anyway, while its ability to replenish supplies in up to six tenders/bunkers at a time was more than was now required for the diminishing steam fleet. The view is looking north – west towards the office block and water tower.

Alongside the office block and with a glimpse of the depot turntable in the background. The latter was of limited diameter and consequently rarely used, in the main, engines being turned on the triangle instead. The sloping shelter gave covered access to the enginemen's lobby and mess room. Originally built as a dormitory and office block, the building ceased to be used for the former purpose likely immediately after the Second World War. No 41299 was one of a number of Ivatt Class 2 tank engines used for shunting and light duties.

A typically filthy Bulleid and hardly clean 'Class 4' and 'U': respectively Nos 34038 *Lynton*, 80016 and 31639. All have arrived back from work and are being disposed before retiring to the shed ready for their next working. Of the three, the tank engine would continue working – it would be on the books at least until 9 July 1967. *Lynton* was withdrawn on 30 June 1966, No 31639 on 6 June. The latter was one of the last two members of the class, both of which were condemned on the same day. (The other 'U' was No 31791.)

Date/Day	Location	Class	Number	Details
		N	31816	Out of steam – inside shed, coupling rods etc removed
		N	31866	In process of being scrapped – not much left
		N	31873	Inside shed
		LM 5	45418	Out of steam inside shed
		LM 2T	41299	In steam alongside coaling stage
		LM 2T	41319	In steam – inside shed
		Stnd 5	73016	Out of steam – rear of shed
		Stnd 5	73083	In steam rear of shed – next to 34008
		Stnd 5	73085	Inside shed
		Stnd 5	73088	Inside shed
		Stnd 5	73117	Inside shed
		Stnd 5	73169	Inside shed
		Stnd 4	75065	Inside shed
		Stnd 4	75075	Entering depot
		Stnd 4	76019	Out of steam – rear of shed
		Stnd 4	76033	Inside shed
		Stnd 4	76061	In steam – alongside coaling stage
		Stnd 4T	80016	Inside shed
		Stnd 4T	80082	Inside shed
		Stnd 4T	80132	In process of being scrapped
		Stnd 4T	80142	Out of steam – rear of shed. See Neg file B, Neg 7
		Stnd 2T	84014	Out of steam – inside shed
		View		Coal stage – showing remains of track ramp
	Eastleigh MPD – Diesel	CL 33'	D6507	
		CL 33'	D6511	
		CL 33'	D6525	
		CL 33'	D6541	
		CL 33'	D6545	
		CL 33'	D6564	
		D'shtr	D2274	
		D'shtr	D2281	Behind 31809
		D'shtr	D3270	
		D'shtr	15201	Withdrawn
		DEMU	1012	

To be continued ….

No 31639 in final condition complete with electrification flashes and AWS. The mess associated with the years of steam is only too apparent; piles of clinker and discarded fire irons, even a former coaling tub, the latter of course now redundant from the coaling stage. In the background are the railway houses in Campbell Road.

Below and opposite top: Two other engines at the coaling stage on the day were 'Standard 4' No 76061 and 'USA' tank No 30064 (which together with No 30071) were receiving attention. The Standard had just over nine months of useful life left, although the two USA tanks would survive until the end, often gainfully employed as works or shed shunters.

Below: **The last active 'Q1', No 33006 officially withdrawn along with sister No 33020 at the end of January 1966 but seen here in steam on 19 March, having just worked the 'LCGB New Forester Railtour' in the area from Eastleigh–Gosport, back to Southampton and thence to Lymington and Brockenhurst. (No 30064 along with 30073 was in charge on the same day for a trip down the Fawley branch). Its work, if any, after 19 March is not certain and the engine was finally taken out of service in April.**

The other 'Q1' No 33020 outside the back of the shed, rods removed 'and not long for this world'. It was in a line of withdrawn engines that included 80142, withdrawn 3 March; 76019, withdrawn 28 March; and 34048 *Crediton*, the last of which was theoretically still on the books and not withdrawn until 31 March, although from its appearance it had already been set aside.

The same line of engines referred to (starting with No 80142) but nearest the shed 34008 *Padstow* and 35023 *Holland Afrika Line*, both of which would survive well into 1967.

No 35023 *Holland Afrika Line* minus rods and temporarily pulled out from inside the shed. (This can be confirmed by the position of the crank pins, which are not all in line.) The engine was in this same position for several days while repairs were effected and was subsequently returned to service to survive until the end of steam.

Another member of the class, No 35030 *Elder Dempster Line,* the last of the class to be built and prophetically also the engine that would haul the very last passenger service train into Waterloo on Sunday, 9 July 1967. It is seen here amongst the debris of the former coaling stage with the ash and coaling crane alongside.

An individual view of No 34008 *Padstow* in filthy condition but still with name and number plates attached. It is outside the back of the shed alongside 'Class 5' No 73083.

Outside the front of the shed in steam was No 34071 *601 Squadron*, then based at Eastleigh and which was also to be its final shed. It was withdrawn from here just over a year later at the end of April 1967.

Finally, and just to prove it was not just steam that was coming to an end, here is one of the trio of SR-built diesel-shunters, No 15201, withdrawn and dumped at the adjacent diesel depot. It had been in the same area since ceasing work back in November 1964, condemned as being non-standard, although as former engineer John Wenyon recounts, ' … the instruction was that as long as the engine was working, they were kept in use: the moment the engine stopped for any reason it was for the chop'.

The
Southern Way

The regular volume for the Southern devotee
MOST RECENT BACK ISSUES

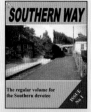

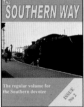

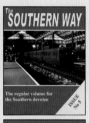

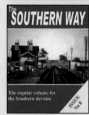

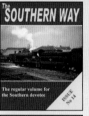

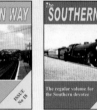

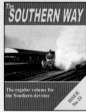
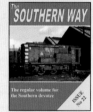

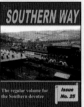
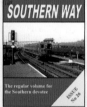
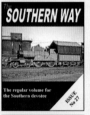

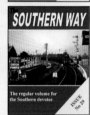

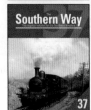

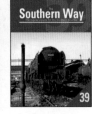
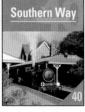
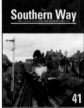